Teach Yourself

VISUALLY™

Investing Online

by Fran Hawthorne

IDG
BOOKS

From

maranGraphics™

IDG Books Worldwide, Inc.
An International Data Group Company
Foster City, CA • Indianapolis • Chicago • New York

Teach Yourself VISUALLY™ Investing Online

Published by
IDG Books Worldwide, Inc.
An International Data Group Company
919 E. Hillsdale Blvd., Suite 400
Foster City, CA 94404
www.idgbooks.com (IDG Books Worldwide Web Site)

Library of Congress Control Number: 00-107550

ISBN: 0-7645-3459-9

Printed in the United States of America
10 9 8 7 6 5 4 3 2 1
1K/TR/QY/QQ/IN
Distributed in the United States by IDG Books Worldwide, Inc.
Distributed by CDG Books Canada Inc. for Canada; by Transworld Publishers
Limited in the United Kingdom; by IDG Norge Books for Norway; by IDG Sweden
Books for Sweden; by Woodslane Pty. Ltd. for Australia; by Woodslane (NZ) Ltd.
for New Zealand; by TransQuest Publishers Pte Ltd. for Singapore, Malaysia,
Thailand, Indonesia, and Hong Kong; by ICG Muse, Inc. for Japan; by Norma
Comunicaciones S.A. for Colombia; by Intersoft for South Africa; by Le Monde
en Tique for France; by International Thomson Publishing for Germany, Austria
and Switzerland; by Distribuidora Cuspide for Argentina; by Livraria Cultura for
Brazil; by Ediciones ZETA S.C.R. Ltda. for Peru; by WS Computer Publishing
Corporation, Inc., for the Philippines; by Contemporanea de Ediciones for
Venezuela; by Express Computer Distributors for the Caribbean and West Indies;
by Micronesia Media Distributor, Inc. for Micronesia; by Grupo Editorial Norma S.A.
for Guatemala; by Chips Computadoras S.A. de C.V. for Mexico; by Editorial Norma
de Panama S.A. for Panama; by American Bookshops for Finland.
For corporate orders, please call maranGraphics at 800-469-6616.
For general information on IDG Books Worldwide's books in the U.S., please call
our Consumer Customer Service department at 800-762-2974.
For reseller information, including discounts and premium sales,
please call our Reseller Customer Service department at 800-434-3422.
For information on where to purchase IDG Books Worldwide's books
outside the U.S., please contact our International Sales department
at 317-572-3993 or fax 317-572-4002.
For consumer information on foreign language translations, please contact
our Customer Service department at 1-800-434-3422, fax 317-572-4002,
or e-mail rights@idgbooks.com.
For information on licensing foreign or domestic rights, please phone 1-650-650-7098.
For sales inquiries and special prices for bulk quantities, please contact
our Order Services department at 800-434-3422.
For information on using IDG Books Worldwide's books in the classroom
or for ordering examination copies, please contact our Educational Sales
department at 800-434-2086 or fax 317-572-4005.
For press review copies, author interviews, or other publicity information, please
contact our Public Relations department at 650-653-7000 or fax 650-653-7500.
For authorization to photocopy items for corporate, personal, or
educational use, please contact Copyright Clearance Center, 222 Rosewood Drive,
Danvers, MA 01923, or fax 978-750-4470.
Screen shots displayed in this book are based on pre-release software
and are subject to change.

Trademark Acknowledgments

is a registered trademark under exclusive
license to IDG Books Worldwide, Inc.
from International Data Group, Inc.

U.S. Corporate Sales	**U.S. Trade Sales**
Contact maranGraphics at (800) 469-6616 or Fax (905) 890-9434.	Contact IDG Books at (800) 434-3422 or (650) 655-3000.

ABOUT IDG BOOKS WORLDWIDE

Welcome to the world of IDG Books Worldwide.

IDG Books Worldwide, Inc., is a subsidiary of International Data Group, the world's largest publisher of computer-related information and the leading global provider of information services on information technology. IDG was founded more than 30 years ago by Patrick J. McGovern and now employs more than 9,000 people worldwide. IDG publishes more than 290 computer publications in over 75 countries. More than 90 million people read one or more IDG publications each month.

Launched in 1990, IDG Books Worldwide is today the #1 publisher of best-selling computer books in the United States. We are proud to have received eight awards from the Computer Press Association in recognition of editorial excellence and three from Computer Currents' First Annual Readers' Choice Awards. Our best-selling ...For Dummies® series has more than 50 million copies in print with translations in 31 languages. IDG Books Worldwide, through a joint venture with IDG's Hi-Tech Beijing, became the first U.S. publisher to publish a computer book in the People's Republic of China. In record time, IDG Books Worldwide has become the first choice for millions of readers around the world who want to learn how to better manage their businesses.

Our mission is simple: Every one of our books is designed to bring extra value and skill-building instructions to the reader. Our books are written by experts who understand and care about our readers. The knowledge base of our editorial staff comes from years of experience in publishing, education, and journalism — experience we use to produce books to carry us into the new millennium. In short, we care about books, so we attract the best people. We devote special attention to details such as audience, interior design, use of icons, and illustrations. And because we use an efficient process of authoring, editing, and desktop publishing our books electronically, we can spend more time ensuring superior content and less time on the technicalities of making books.

You can count on our commitment to deliver high-quality books at competitive prices on topics you want to read about. At IDG Books Worldwide, we continue in the IDG tradition of delivering quality for more than 30 years. You'll find no better book on a subject than one from IDG Books Worldwide.

John Kilcullen
Chairman and CEO
IDG Books Worldwide, Inc.

Eighth Annual Computer Press Awards ≥1992

Ninth Annual Computer Press Awards ≥1993

Tenth Annual Computer Press Awards ≥1994

Eleventh Annual Computer Press Awards ≥1995

IDG is the world's leading IT media, research and exposition company. Founded in 1964, IDG had 1997 revenues of $2.05 billion and has more than 9,000 employees worldwide. IDG offers the widest range of media options that reach IT buyers in 75 countries representing 95% of worldwide IT spending. IDG's diverse product and services portfolio spans six key areas including print publishing, online publishing, expositions and conferences, market research, education and training, and global marketing services. More than 90 million people read one or more of IDG's 290 magazines and newspapers, including IDG's leading global brands — Computerworld, PC World, Network World, Macworld and the Channel World family of publications. IDG Books Worldwide is one of the fastest-growing computer book publishers in the world, with more than 700 titles in 36 languages. The "...For Dummies®" series alone has more than 50 million copies in print. IDG offers online users the largest network of technology-specific Web sites around the world through IDG.net (http://www.idg.net), which comprises more than 225 targeted Web sites in 55 countries worldwide. International Data Corporation (IDC) is the world's largest provider of information technology data, analysis and consulting, with research centers in over 41 countries and more than 400 research analysts worldwide. IDG World Expo is a leading producer of more than 168 globally branded conferences and expositions in 35 countries including E3 (Electronic Entertainment Expo), Macworld Expo, ComNet, Windows World Expo, ICE (Internet Commerce Expo), Agenda, DEMO, and Spotlight. IDG's training subsidiary, ExecuTrain, is the world's largest computer training company, with more than 230 locations worldwide and 785 training courses. IDG Marketing Services helps industry-leading IT companies build international brand recognition by developing global integrated marketing programs via IDG's print, online and exposition products worldwide. Further information about the company can be found at www.idg.com.
                                                                                                                    1/26/00

maranGraphics is a family-run business
located near Toronto, Canada.

At **maranGraphics**, we believe in producing great computer books — one book at a time.

maranGraphics has been producing high-technology products for over 25 years, which enables us to offer the computer book community a unique communication process.

Our computer books use an integrated communication process, which is very different from the approach used in other computer books. Each spread is, in essence, a flow chart — the text and screen shots are totally incorporated into the layout of the spread. Introductory text and helpful tips complete the learning experience.

maranGraphics' approach encourages the left and right sides of the brain to work together — resulting in faster orientation and greater memory retention.

Above all, we are very proud of the handcrafted nature of our books. Our carefully-chosen writers are experts in their fields, and spend countless hours researching and organizing the content for each topic. Our artists rebuild every screen shot to provide the best clarity possible, making our screen shots the most precise and easiest to read in the industry. We strive for perfection, and believe that the time spent handcrafting each element results in the best computer books money can buy.

Thank you for purchasing this book. We hope you enjoy it!

Sincerely,

Robert Maran
President
maranGraphics
Rob@maran.com
www.maran.com
www.idgbooks.com/visual

CREDITS

Acquisitions, Editorial, and Media Development

Project Editor
Dana Rhodes Lesh

Acquisitions Editor
Martine Edwards

Associate Project Coordinator
Lindsay Sandman

Senior Copy Editor
Ted Cains

Proof Editor
Dwight Ramsey

Technical Editor
Adam Bergman

Permissions Editor
Carmen Krikorian

Editorial Manager
Rev Mengle

Media Development Manager
Heather Heath Dismore

Editorial Assistant:
Candace Nicholson

Production

Book Design
maranGraphics™

Project Coordinator
Valery Bourke

Layout
Joe Bucki, Barry Offringa, Kathie Schutte

Proofreaders:
Laura Albert, Marianne Santy,
York Production Services, Inc.

Indexer:
York Production Services, Inc.

Special Help:
Craig Dearing

ACKNOWLEDGMENTS

General and Administrative

IDG Books Worldwide, Inc.: John Kilcullen, CEO

IDG Books Technology Publishing Group: Richard Swadley, Senior Vice President and Publisher; Walter R. Bruce III, Vice President and Publisher; Joseph Wikert, Vice President and Publisher; Mary Bednarek, Vice President and Director, Product Development; Andy Cummings, Publishing Director, General User Group; Mary C. Corder, Editorial Director; Barry Pruett, Publishing Director

IDG Books Consumer Publishing Group: Roland Elgey, Senior Vice President and Publisher; Kathleen A. Welton, Vice President and Publisher; Kevin Thornton, Acquisitions Manager; Kristin A. Cocks, Editorial Director

IDG Books Internet Publishing Group: Brenda McLaughlin, Senior Vice President and Publisher; Sofia Marchant, Online Marketing Manager

IDG Books Production for Branded Press: Debbie Stailey, Director of Production; Cindy L. Phipps, Manager of Project Coordination, Production Proofreading, and Indexing; Tony Augsburger, Manager of Prepress, Reprints, and Systems; Shelley Lea, Supervisor of Graphics and Design; Debbie J. Gates, Production Systems Specialist; Robert Springer, Supervisor of Proofreading; Trudy Coler, Page Layout Manager; Kathie Schutte, Senior Page Layout Supervisor; Janet Seib, Page Layout Supervisor; Michael Sullivan, Production Supervisor

Packaging and Book Design: Patty Page, Manager, Promotions Marketing

The publisher would like to give special thanks to Patrick J. McGovern,
without whom this book would not have been possible.

ABOUT THE AUTHOR

Fran Hawthorne has spent more than 20 years covering business and finance as an editor and writer at *Fortune, Business Week,* and *Institutional Investor* magazines. In that time, she's watched the birth and growth of the Internet, personal computers, 401(k) plans, life-cycle mutual funds and Silicon Valley, among other trends. She lives in New York City with her husband and three children.

AUTHOR ACKNOWLEDGMENTS

I would like to thank the following people for seeing me through countless trivial questions, computer breakdowns and general anxiety:

Christopher Cordaro of Bugen, Stuart, Korn & Cordaro

Wrolf Courtney

Ross Levin of Accredited Investors

Portia Richardson

Diane Savage of Watson Wyatt Worldwide

At IDG: Dana Lesh, Martine Edwards, Carmen Krikorian, Adam Bergman, Ted Cains, and Lindsay Sandman

And most of all, Pete Segal, my husband and "tech support," and our children, Mallory, Lauren, and Joey

TABLE OF CONTENTS

Chapter 3

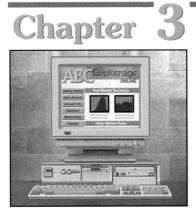

CHOOSING AN ONLINE BROKER

Chapter 4

TRADING STOCKS ONLINE

TABLE OF CONTENTS

Chapter 5

Chapter 6

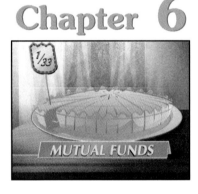

Chapter 7

Chapter 8

Chapter 9

TABLE OF CONTENTS

Chapter 12

NOW A WORD ABOUT DAY TRADING

CHAPTER 1

Taking Your Investments Online

How do you handle financial transactions on the Internet, and how do you know that they're safe? How does your broker's Web site talk to your bank? This chapter takes you step by step onto the Internet and helps prepare you to invest online.

UNDERSTAND HOW ONLINE INVESTING WORKS

On the Internet, you can perform almost any financial transaction you can name: You can trade stocks and bonds, pay bills, transfer money between bank accounts, and even buy artwork.

Essentially, the Internet is a method of communication. And in order to perform financial transactions over the Internet, companies need a way to communicate information that each may store or code differently on its own site.

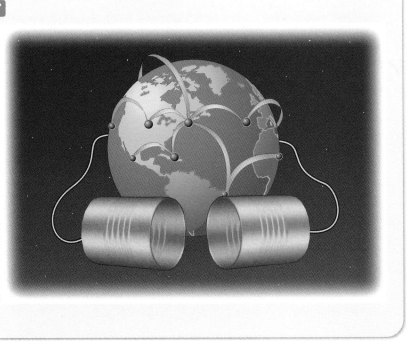

OPEN FINANCIAL EXCHANGE

Open Financial Exchange (OFX) is the standard that most banks, brokerages, and other companies use today to share financial information electronically. To take one of the technical terms, it is a *common data interface.* The technology involves the way data is stored as well as transmitted.

OFX was developed in 1997 by three of the biggest online financial providers: Microsoft, Intuit, and CheckFree.

For the business world, OFX involves an unusual amount of cooperation among rivals.

A COMMON LANGUAGE

Think of it this way: If you want to pay your utility bill online, you need to tell your bank to send a certain amount of money to the utility company. Then the bank has to communicate that information to the utility company. Finally, the utility company has to credit your account.

In a world without a standard like OFX, it would be as though you spoke English, your bank kept its records in French, and the utility company kept its records in Chinese. To make matters worse, you would be trying to send your message to the bank by mail, but your bank would be able to understand messages only in Morse code.

KEEP YOUR SECRETS SAFE

If your first question about investing online is "Is my money safe on the Internet?," then the answer is simple: Yes, it is exceedingly safe. Millions of dollars flow in and out of bank accounts, stocks, mutual funds, and bonds every day online, and they're all protected by layers on layers of codes, keys, passwords, and other forms of security.

SECURE SOCKETS LAYER

The Internet system that keeps sensitive information secure is called *SSL*, or *secure sockets layer*. SSL involves two different sets of complex computer coding—RSA and DES, which are discussed in the following two sections.

TWO SETS OF KEYS

Most transactions start with *RSA encryption.* (*RSA* stands for *Rivest-Shamir-Adleman,* the developers who came up with the encryption algorithm.)

The financial institution sends customers a *public key* to use in encrypting their information. This key is created by multiplying two very large prime numbers. Because it is extraordinarily difficult to do this in reverse—to split a very large number back down to the two original factors, or numbers—it is almost impossible for an outsider to decode the message. Only the financial institution has the *private* decoder key—the original two numbers.

Each time a customer starts a new transaction, a new set of keys is created.

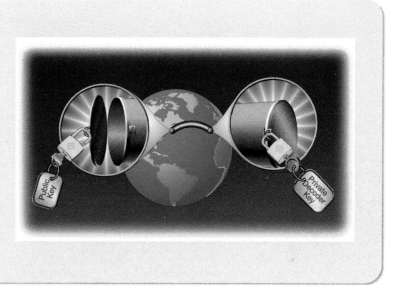

A SECOND CODE

The RSA system is extremely secure. But because it is very slow and requires a lot of computing power, it does not work well for long messages.

That's where the second part of SSL comes in. The bulk of a transaction is encrypted with a much simpler *Data Encryption Standard (DES) code,* which is based on codes used in World War II. The RSA code is used only once, at the beginning of a transaction, to send the customer the key for the DES code.

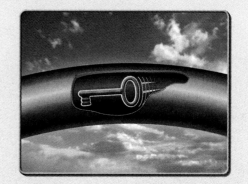

CAN THE CODE BE BROKEN?

Some very powerful computers have managed to break a public key RSA number into the two original prime numbers. But it takes a rare kind of super-high-speed computer to do it. And more powerful types of RSA codes have not been broken. You can feel secure knowing that your financial transactions on the Internet are still extremely safe.

Chapter 11 goes into more detail about ways to protect the security of your Internet financial transactions.

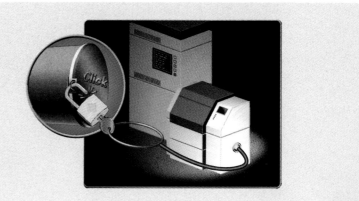

EXPLORE THE ADVANTAGES OF INVESTING ONLINE

At the turn of the millennium, more than 9 million people were using online brokers, trading over half a million shares a day. For these Web surfers, investing online is practical, efficient—and probably fun.

CONVENIENCE

With just a few clicks on a mouse or keyboard, you may now own a thousand shares of stock. You don't have to drive to a broker's office, wait endlessly on hold on the telephone, or write a letter.

In fact, you never have to leave home! You can trade thousands of dollars in your pajamas.

Moreover, you can combine banking, stock trading, and budgeting in one account.

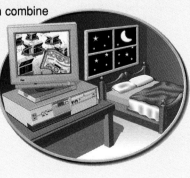

INFORMATION

To get the kind of information that is available through the Web, you would have to spend hours in the library or write to your broker for piles of brochures—and even then you would not have as much information as you can get with a few keystrokes.

SPEED

After you punch in your message, you typically get results within minutes or even seconds. That way, you can immediately find out if your trade went through and at what price. You also have a better chance of getting in at the price you want.

AROUND-THE-CLOCK ACCESS

What is the definition of *business hours* these days? With the Internet, when you work or sleep or even what hours the markets are open doesn't matter. Although you may not be able to trade stocks all day and night, you can be online at 2 a.m. if you want, studying recent stock price movements, picking up gossip in a chat room, registering with an auction service, and generally surfing for financial information.

LOWER COST

Because you can book your trade as soon as you see a price movement, you may be able to lock in lower prices by going online. Even if not, at least you can save on the peripheral costs, such as stamps or gas. Many online brokers are also offering incentives to bring in new customers.

Online investing is not for everyone. You have to be a do-it-yourselfer, knowledgeable about finance, and comfortable tackling both technology and investing.

TOO MUCH INFORMATION

When you go online, you have access to hundreds of Web sites offering financial information. Each of them has numerous subcategories and perhaps links to other sites. Because these sites never shut down at night, you could spend all your waking hours—and some hours that you should be sleeping—staring at a computer screen. Eventually, you could suffer from information overload.

You have to be able to screen out the crucial information from the frills.

"SHORT-TERMITIS"

Because you can get up-to-date information about your finances whenever you want, you may be tempted to constantly log on. Naturally, you will want to see how the stock market has moved since the last time you checked. If there's been a lot of change, you may start buying or selling in a panic.

In short, you could succumb to "short-termitis"—paying too much attention to short-term movements.

NO PERSONAL CONTACT

If you are a sociable person, you may miss the chance to talk on the phone or in person to a live human being. Getting your questions answered online may also be harder.

Most important: Many people need advice in picking their investments. Some online financial providers do offer advice, but many stress no-frills trading only. Chapter 3 explains the range of services online brokers provide in more detail.

TECHNICAL PROBLEMS

When you have a complex, sophisticated system that depends on numerous different sources, something is bound to break down eventually: Your Internet connection may crash, your computer may become outdated, a Web site's server can go down, and so on.

Chapters 3 and 11 cover technical problems and how to handle them in more detail.

ARE YOU READY FOR INVESTING ONLINE?

If you're not familiar with the Internet, it can seem intimidating—so much information, so many things to click. And if you're going to be handling investments online, your money is at stake.

TEST YOURSELF

To see if you're ready to leap into the world of online investing, take the test on the following page. If you answer yes to three or fewer questions, you should think seriously about whether investing over the Internet is the right way for you to invest just now. The information in this book may help you prepare to be ready. If you answer yes to four or five of the questions, go ahead and try investing online—but do not manage too much of your money this way. And if you answer yes to six or more of the questions, you should be very happy typing away on your keyboard!

1. Do you handle most of your own investment decisions even without using the Internet?

2. When you see a new gadget advertised, are you eager to get it?

3. Do you like to collect raw information yourself, rather than read someone else's analysis of it?

4. Do you feel comfortable making decisions yourself?

5. Do you like to try new things?

6. Do you have more than two significant hobbies or interests?

7. Do you use a computer just about every day at work, school, or home? (Give yourself half credit if you use a computer at least three days a week.)

8. Do you use the Internet more than three times a week, even if it's not for financial topics? (Give yourself half credit if you use the Internet at least once a week regularly.)

Bonus Question: Do you travel a lot?

ABOUT THE BONUS QUESTION: A TRAVELER'S AIDE

How does frequent traveling affect your online finances? Well, if you're away from home at least three days a week or for a couple weeks at a time, you should probably set up automatic online bill paying. That way you can bring your laptop with you and do your banking on the road, rather than come home to a house full of bills. You can find a fuller explanation of online banking in Chapter 9.

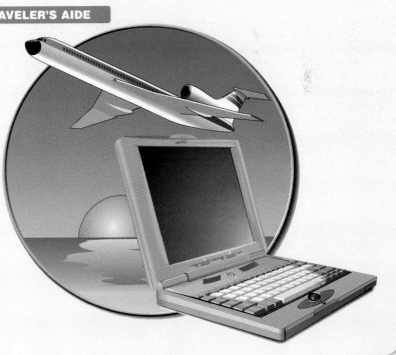

ACCESS THE NET: USING AN INTERNET SERVICE PROVIDER

An *Internet service provider*—or *ISP*—is a company that gives you access to the Internet for a modest fee or sometimes for free. Two popular ISPs are Earthlink and America Online.

WHAT YOU GET

One way to look at an ISP is to compare it to a phone company. The phone company connects your phone to a network that ultimately hooks you up with other people's phones. An ISP connects you to a network—the Internet—that connects you to other people's computers, plus a world of information sources.

The ISPs with monthly fees generally offer more features—and fewer banner ads—than free ones. Most ISPs give customers e-mail capability, and some have a screening service that blocks certain types of information, such as unwanted junk mail. AOL provides chat rooms, weather maps, and news.

CHOOSING AN ISP

You have two basic options when selecting your Internet service provider: a national ISP, such as AOL, the Microsoft Network (MSN), or AT&T WorldNet, or a local ISP that serves only your region. National ISPs often have special channels or services but tend to cost more. Local ISPs are usually less expensive and may have services that are community-oriented, such as listings of local events.

To find a local ISP, you can check the "Internet Services" or "Internet" section of your local yellow pages. Or you can look through your local newspaper's business pages for ads from ISPs. Your best option may be to ask your friends what service providers they use.

CONNECTING TO YOUR ISP

To connect to the Internet via an ISP, you'll need a device called a *modem* attached to your regular telephone line (unless you use one of the faster connection methods discussed in the "Faster Access" section). The first time you try to connect to the Internet, follow the instructions your ISP gave you and use the software it provided when you signed up.

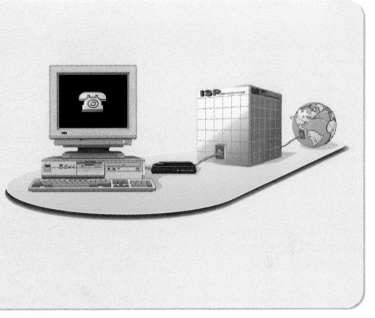

When you dial in, you hear a dial tone and a series of beeps as your computer dials the ISP and connects. You may even see a little picture of a telephone on your screen. Just as with a phone, you may get a busy signal. Your ISP should provide you with alternative local phone numbers to use in case this happens.

Modems are still the most commonly used method of connecting to the Internet.

FASTER ACCESS

Some speedier methods of connecting, called *high bandwidth* or *broadband*, are starting to become widely available. Among other things, they promise to make it easier to send video, audio, and complex graphics. These systems connect you to the Internet via cable or special phone lines known as a Digital Subscriber Line (DSL) or an Integrated Systems Digital Network (ISDN).

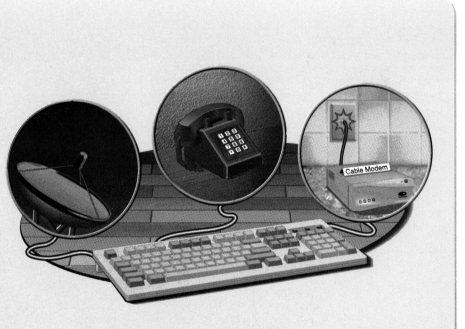

Of course, each of these methods has its own disadvantages, mainly cost, limited range, and security concerns. And some may not be available where you live.

ACCESS THE NET WITH A WEB BROWSER

If an ISP can be compared to a phone company, then a Web browser is your voice asking the long-distance operator to connect you. In other words, a *Web browser* is software that provides you with a way to request and display information from the Net.

The two most common Web browsers are Microsoft Internet Explorer and Netscape Navigator.

HOW TO ASK FOR INFORMATION

A browser requests the information you want by calling up the address of the Web site page where it's located. Web sites are simply a collection of computer files, each with its own unique address, known as its *URL*, or *Universal Resource Locator*. Each URL consists of a series of letters, punctuation marks, and perhaps numbers.

Most URLs begin with `http://` and end with `.com` (commercial sites), `.org` (nonprofit organizations and now some commercial sites), `.gov` (government sites), or `.edu` (educational sites).

6 Elm St.

THE HOME PAGE

The first thing that appears on your screen when you start your browser is your *home page*. Often, your home page is your ISP's Web site, but you can change it to be any Web page you want. You'll want to use a home page that serves as a good jumping-off point to browse the Web; the standard ones provided by ISPs usually come with a whole range of information, from links to other Web sites, to news headlines, to ways of getting football scores. But you can usually customize your home page to include the kinds of information you would like right at hand.

Don't be confused if you hear the term *home page* used differently. A Web site's main Web page (the first page you see when you visit a site) is also called its *home page*.

BOOKMARKS AND FAVORITES

Most browsers let you save the addresses of Web sites you frequently visit so that you can easily return to them without retyping the whole address. Those saved addresses are called *bookmarks* or *favorites*.

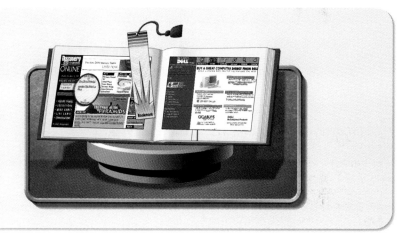

DIFFERENT SPEEDS

True, some browsers load pages faster or slower than others. But it may not always be the browser's fault. Web pages load at different speeds, depending on the complexity of the information to be displayed—especially if the page contains a lot of detailed color graphics or audio. How fast pages load also depends on the speed of your Internet connection.

USING A WEB BROWSER

A typical browser lets you visit sites, remember where you have been, and manipulate the Web in various ways.

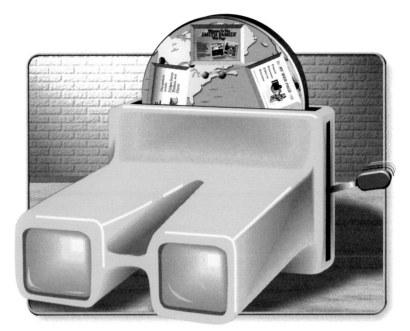

USING MICROSOFT INTERNET EXPLORER

■ What results when you click Favorites

1 Click **Favorites** to access favorite sites that you have marked so that you can find them easily.

2 Click **Mail** for e-mail options.

3 To access a particular Web site, type its URL here.

■ What results when you click History

4 Click **History** for a list of sites that you have visited recently.

5 Click **Search** to perform a search.

6 Click **Refresh** to reload the page you are reading.

What if I have forgotten the exact URL that I once used and I never bookmarked it?

Luckily, most browsers have a great memory. As soon as you start typing the first key word of the URL, the browser often finishes the address for you.

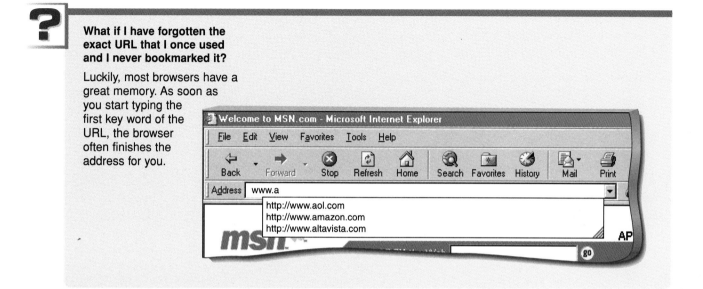

USING NETSCAPE NAVIGATOR

1 Click **Bookmarks** to access favorite sites thay you have marked so that you can find them easily.

2 Click **Reload** to reload the page you're visiting.

3 Click **Search** to perform a search.

■ This is Netscape's default portal, but you can customize it.

4 Click **New and Cool** to access sites and news tidbits that Netscape has selected.

5 To access a particular Web site, type its URL in the Go To box.

6 Click **Netcaster** for a service that enables you to receive constant on-screen updates about subjects of your choice while you are doing other work.

7 Click **Look Up** to find addresses for companies and people.

USING A SEARCH ENGINE

A search engine helps you quickly find Web sites. You can search the Web by entering a keyword or keywords: The search engines look for sites that contain your keywords from the long lists of sites that they maintain.

Two popular search engines are AltaVista (www.altavista.com) and Direct Hit (www.directhit.com).

USING A SEARCH ENGINE

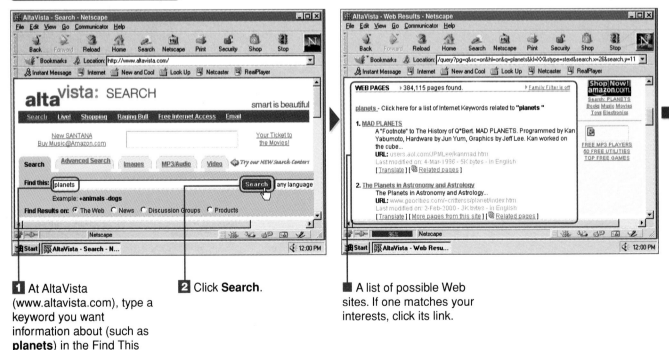

1 At AltaVista (www.altavista.com), type a keyword you want information about (such as **planets**) in the Find This box.

2 Click **Search**.

■ A list of possible Web sites. If one matches your interests, click its link.

What if the search engine comes up with thousands of sites?

You should try to narrow your search as much as possible. Don't ask for just "pyramid" if you're looking for the pyramids near Cairo. Type multiple keywords (separated by just a space), enclose groups of words in quotation marks, or ask a complete question. You can also place a plus sign in front of words that must appear on the page or a minus sign in front of words you don't want.

Egypt Pyramid Cairo
SPACE

"Egyptian Pyramids"
QUOTATION MARKS

Who created the pyramids?
QUESTION

Egypt+Pyramid-Sphinx
PLUS SIGN AND MINUS SIGN

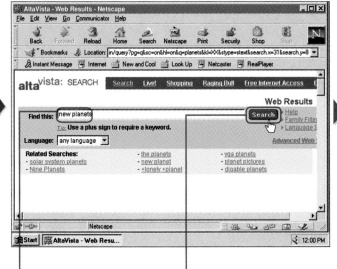

3 Type another, narrower set of keywords (such as **new planets**) in the Find This box.

4 Click **Search**.

■ A new list of possible Web sites comes up. Again, if one matches your interests, click its link.

5 Click **Answer** to get a news story that answers the question AltaVista guesses you may ask.

USING A PORTAL

Portal means door, and that is exactly what an Internet portal aims to be—your doorway to the Web. Portals have fast, easy-to-access links directly to a range of Web sites, so you don't need to type or even know a particular URL. Many people even set up their favorite portal as their browser's home page.

In seeking out Web sites, a portal is similar to a search engine, but it organizes Web sites by categories rather than keyword to help you find specific topics you're interested in.

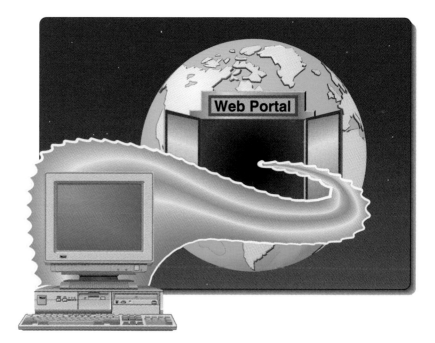

USING THE YAHOO! PORTAL

1 At Yahoo! (www.yahoo.com), click **Finance** to get a range of financial information – everything from stock prices to headlines.

2 On the next page, click **Yahoo! Finance**.

3 Click one of the subjects after U.S. Markets, such as **Major U.S. Indices**, to get more details.

Do I always have to go through all these steps on Yahoo!?

No. After you have gone through the steps once and found a URL you like, you can bookmark the page.

4 Click **Chart** or **News** to view a history of a stock's recent price movements and other headlines about the stock.

■ Of course, you can use Yahoo! to research any topic, not just financial subjects. If you go back to the Yahoo! home page and type **Dr. Seuss** in the search box, you get the results in this figure.

■ Category matches

■ Related Web sites

CONTINUED

A portal showers you with all sorts of information—prepackaged information, such as headlines, as well as do-it-yourself data, such as your local weather forecast.

USING THE EXCITE PORTAL

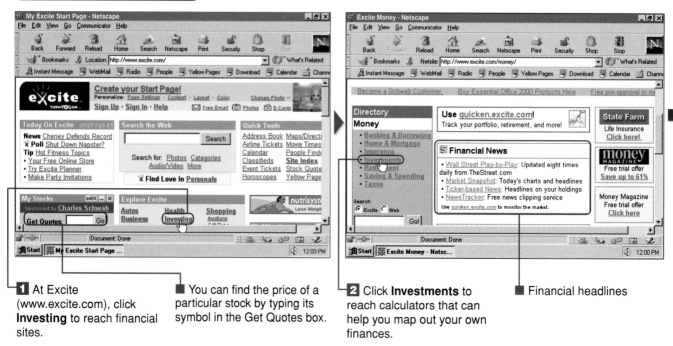

1 At Excite (www.excite.com), click **Investing** to reach financial sites.

■ You can find the price of a particular stock by typing its symbol in the Get Quotes box.

2 Click **Investments** to reach calculators that can help you map out your own finances.

■ Financial headlines

I like two different portals for different reasons. Do I have to choose one?

You can use two or 20 portals—as long as you do not try to run two searches at the same time. You do not have to sign up or become a member.

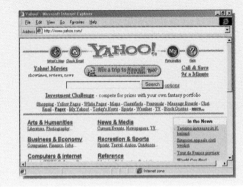 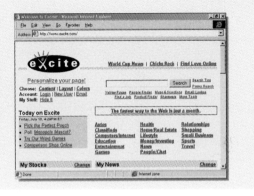

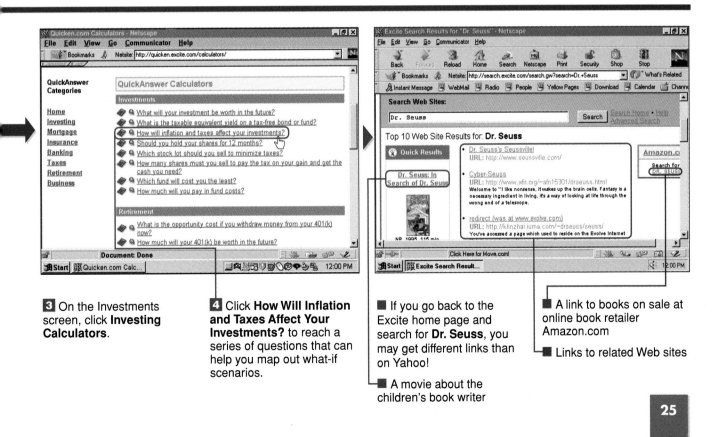

3 On the Investments screen, click **Investing Calculators**.

4 Click **How Will Inflation and Taxes Affect Your Investments?** to reach a series of questions that can help you map out what-if scenarios.

■ If you go back to the Excite home page and search for **Dr. Seuss**, you may get different links than on Yahoo!

■ A movie about the children's book writer

■ A link to books on sale at online book retailer Amazon.com

■ Links to related Web sites

GET YOUR FEET WET

You would not go straight from riding a tricycle to racing in the Indy 500. So how can you expect to jump from paper stock certificates and checks to shooting all your hard-earned money through the ether, in just one move?

Forget investing for the moment. You need to get comfortable with the idea of using the Internet. When you have a few spare moments, poke around Web sites on nonfinancial topics you are interested in. Get familiar with typing in URL addresses and using links. Because you are not risking any money and are reading about topics you like, you may actually come to enjoy being online.

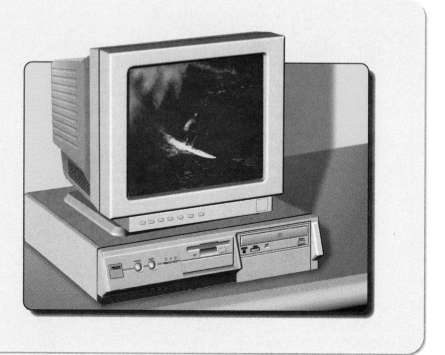

PRACTICE, PRACTICE, PRACTICE

A number of financial sites offer practice portfolios, mock financial modeling, and other dress rehearsals, which you can access as often as you like. For example, you can try your hand at pretending to pay bills, transfer money between bank accounts, and do other banking tasks electronically through the Test Drive function on Citibank's Web site (www.citibank.com) and the Demo function at American Express's banking site (www.american express.com/ banking).

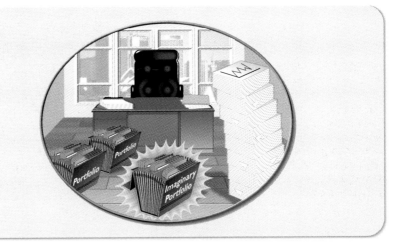

CHAT ABOUT YOUR TECH ANXIETY

Put your qualms to practical use: Log on to a chat room and find others who share your trepidation. That way, you can practice communicating online while getting advice and sympathy on the very topic of practicing online.

START SLOWLY

Financial planner Diane Savage of Watson Wyatt Worldwide suggests that you start with partial steps. For instance, you may want to put some money in an online brokerage account, but keep most of your assets with your old broker.

If you are worried about security and privacy, you could do just your banking on the Web for starters. "I don't care if anyone sees my checking account balance," Savage says. "What are they going to get from that?" Later, when you're more comfortable with online finances, you can move on to trading stocks, which probably involves a lot more money.

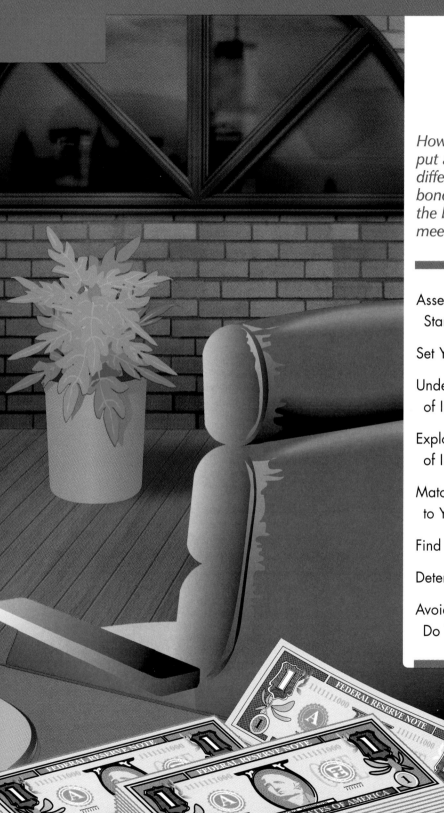

CHAPTER 2

Drawing Your Financial Portrait

How much money can you afford to put aside for investing? What is the difference between a stock and a bond? This chapter helps you select the best kinds of investments for meeting your goals.

ASSESS WHERE YOU'RE STARTING FROM

Before you go on a trip to a new place, you probably map out your route. The same goes for planning your investment journey: You need to find the best way to get from where you are now to where you want to go.

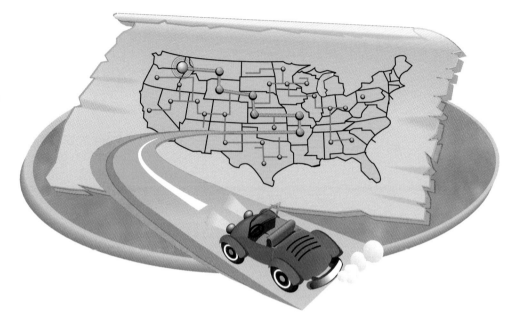

ANNUAL EXPENSES

Write down your best estimate of how much you spend every year. You can write your answers in the space provided here or on a separate sheet of paper.

Rent/mortgage _____

Household maintenance (repairs, cleaning, gardening) _____

Utilities, phone _____

Food _____

School/babysitting/camp _____

Medical _____

Transportation (car payments, gas and upkeep, fees, parking, mass transit) _____

Dues and contributions (union, religious organization, club, sports) _____

ANNUAL EXPENSES (CONTINUED)

Clothing and cleaning   _____

Furniture   _____

Insurance (car, house, life, medical)   _____

Taxes   _____

Loan payments/alimony/child support/credit card finance charges   _____

Parents' care   _____

Computer, ISP fee   _____

401(k), IRA, college plan contributions   _____

Entertainment (books, movies, cable TV, dining out, vacation)   _____

Other (Gifts, beauty parlor, postage, toys, music lessons, pets, hobbies, cigarettes, and so on)   _____

TOTAL ANNUAL EXPENSES: _____

Tip: (from financial planner Christopher Cordaro of Bugen, Stuart, Korn, & Cordaro in Chatham, New Jersey): "The hardest part is figuring out what you're actually spending. Take one day, and try to keep track of everything you buy."

After you finish calculating your annual expenses, try to estimate your annual income. Then see which is bigger. And be tough on yourself: Underestimate your income a little if you are not sure of the exact amount.

ANNUAL INCOME

Write down your best estimate of how much you earn every year. You can write your answers in the space provided here or on a separate sheet of paper.

Salary and wages _____

Bonus _____

Commission _____

Interest _____

Dividends _____

Partnerships and royalties _____

Real estate/rental income _____

Trust income _____

ANNUAL INCOME (CONTINUED)

Exercise of stock options (if recurring) _____

Pension, Social Security, disability, public
assistance, alimony, child support _____

Other (odd jobs, freelance work, and so on) _____

TOTAL ANNUAL INCOME: _____

One-Time Windfalls

You can give yourself a little credit for windfalls under the Other
column in the Annual Income checklist.

Awards and prizes _____

Legacies and gifts _____

Proceeds from sale of assets
(including tag sales) _____

Tip: For some online planners that help
you calculate income and expenses
specifically for retirement planning, see
Chapter 10.

SET YOUR FINANCIAL GOALS

Maybe you've daydreamed that you'd like to retire before you turn 65, or you expect your kids to go to college. Have you thought about what that kind of goal really involves?

YOUR GOALS

Write down your best estimate of how much each of your goals will cost, when you will need the money, and how much you can afford to set aside for these costs. You can write your answers in the space provided here or on a separate sheet of paper.

Home purchase or renovation:

Price range   _____

Anticipated date   _____

Down payment you'll need (including closing costs) in the year 20__   _____

Annual payments after the first year   _____

How much you can realistically afford to set aside for this goal
(based on the difference between your annual expenses and income)   _____

College:

Number of children   _____

Starting date   _____

Number of years it is expected to last   _____

Expected annual cost per child (including tuition, fees, books, living expenses)   _____

Amount you'll need in the year 20__   _____

Annual payment schedule   _____

How much you can realistically afford to set aside for this goal
(based on the difference between your annual expenses and income)   _____

YOUR GOALS (CONTINUED)

Retirement:

Anticipated date _____

Desired income _____

Expected income _____

Current income _____

Income shortfall as of the year 20__ _____

How much you can realistically afford to set aside for this goal
(based on the difference between your annual expenses and income) _____

Medical treatment:

Expected unreimbursed cost _____

Anticipated date _____

Payment schedule (how much due before treatment, at treatment, afterwards) _____

Amount you'll need as of the year 20__ _____

How much you can realistically afford to set aside for this goal
(based on the difference between your annual expenses and income) _____

Family vacation:

Anticipated date _____

Expected fixed costs (airfare, hotel, tour group) _____

Expected variable costs (souvenirs, food) _____

Payment schedule (size of the deposit and when it is due, when the balance is due) _____

Amount you'll need as of the year 20__ _____

How much you can realistically afford to set aside for this goal
(based on the difference between your annual expenses and income) _____

Other:

Expected cost _____

How soon _____

Amount you'll need in the year 20__ _____

How much you can realistically afford to set aside for this goal
(based on the difference between your annual expenses and income) _____

SOME ASSUMPTIONS

Between now and the year you need to start paying for your
goal, how much do you expect the following to change:

- **Interest rates:** Up/down __%

- **Inflation:** Up/down __%

- **Stock market/other investment returns:** Up/down __%

Tip: Of course, no one can predict the future. But, based on historical trends, most experts assume an inflation rate of 3 percent. And depending on your mix of investments, you should probably figure on an investment return between 8 percent and 10 percent.

UNDERSTAND THE BASICS OF INVESTMENT

You can invest in lots of different ways, but whichever you choose, you should follow these four basic principles: using money to make money, risk and return, diversification, and taking a long-term view.

USING MONEY TO MAKE MONEY

SAVING VERSUS INVESTING

The first step toward reaching your financial goal is to safeguard your money instead of spending it. You could put it under your mattress, in a piggy bank, or in a bank account. If you do that, you are *saving*.

But if you put $5 in a piggy bank, at the end of a year all you have is still just $5. It would be even better if you could use that money to make more money. That is the basic idea behind investing. *Investing* is different from saving in two significant ways: Instead of simply putting money aside, you try to make that pool of money bigger, and you take some risk in doing so.

USING MONEY TO MAKE MONEY (CONTINUED)

INVESTING VERSUS GAMBLING

How is investing any different from gambling? In both cases, you are taking a chance. You have no guarantee that you will make money or even keep the money you start out with.

But when you invest, you can take some steps to tilt the odds in your favor. You can research your investments thoroughly. You can choose stocks that are riskier or less risky. When you gamble, by contrast, you have almost no control over what happens. The odds favor the house, and whether you draw a royal flush or 21 is purely a matter of luck.

Further, with a single bet, you face an all-or-nothing proposition: You either win or lose all your money based on one outcome. However, if you place that same amount of money in an investment, you may lose or gain money incrementally. That gives you a chance to change your mind.

RISK AND RETURN

RISK AND RETURN

Every investment involves risk. You could lose all your money. On the other hand, you are hoping that you will make a lot more money.

The other side of risk is return. The bigger the risk, the bigger the return should be.

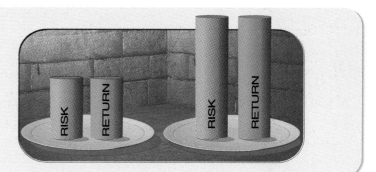

TYPES OF RISK

The most well-known type of investment risk is called *beta*, or risk that affects the stock market as a whole. For instance, just about all investments would be hurt if inflation really jumped.

Beyond that, the company you invest in probably faces other risks, depending on its size and type of business. Small or new companies are generally riskier than big or established ones, because you cannot be sure that they will stay in business.

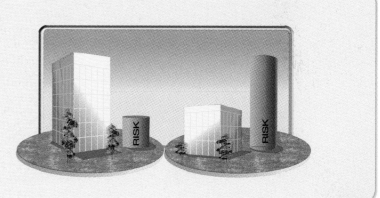

To keep your risk low and your return high, just remember one word: *diversify*.

DIVERSIFICATION

DIVERSIFYING

The best way to protect your investments is to spread the risk.

Investment professionals have an old saying that asset allocation accounts for 90 percent of your return. *Asset allocation* means spreading—or allocating—your money among a range of different sorts of investments, such as stocks, bonds, and real estate. These investments are described in the section "Explore the Different Types of Investments."

AND DIVERSIFYING AGAIN

After you allocate your assets among various types of investments, you should diversify again within each type. If you are buying stocks, do not just buy the stocks of big, established, American consumer-goods companies, for example. You should buy both large- and small-company stocks, U.S. and non-U.S. companies, and new and established businesses.

LONG-TERM THINKING

THE LONG-TERM VIEW

You could buy a stock today, and it may drop tomorrow. If you hold onto the stock for a year, it could go up and down several times. But studies have shown that over the long term—say, 15 years or more—stocks usually rise in value.

So you need to have patience!

Besides, if you are saving for a particular goal, it is probably a long way off in the future.

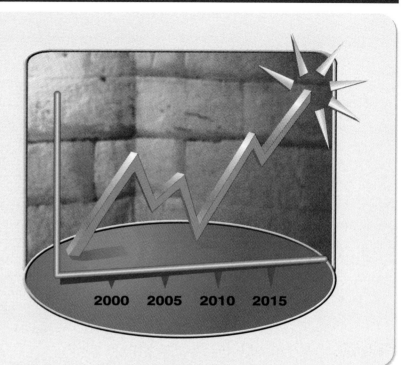

2000   2005   2010   2015

YOU DO NOT HAVE TO HOLD A STOCK FOREVER

Having patience does not mean you should never sell an investment. You should give a stock or other holding a reasonable chance—perhaps six months, perhaps a year, perhaps five years, depending on the situation.

But if the price keeps falling, and all the indications are that the company is not solving its problems, then it is reasonable to stop being patient and start selling.

EXPLORE THE DIFFERENT TYPES OF INVESTMENTS

Investments come in a wide range of varieties. They have different levels of risk, different maturities, different structures, and of course, very different returns.

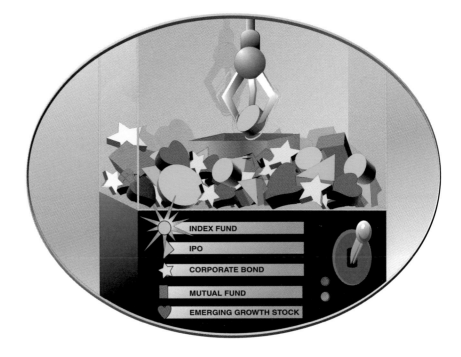

INDEX FUND

IPO

CORPORATE BOND

MUTUAL FUND

EMERGING GROWTH STOCK

BONDS

A *bond* is really just an IOU: When you buy a bond, you are lending money to a company or government, which promises to pay you back, with interest, on a set schedule. You can find out more about bonds in Chapter 5.

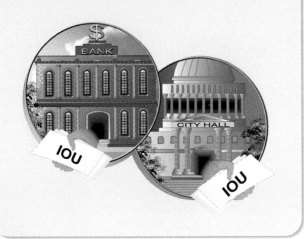

STOCKS

A *stock* is a piece of a company. Owning a share of stock literally means you are one of the owners of the company. Of course, it is not exactly like owning your own business. There are thousands of other owners just like you, each with just a tiny stake. You can find out more about stocks in Chapter 4.

IPOS

An *IPO—initial public offering—* involves a certain kind of stock holding. It marks the first time a company has sold stock to the public. Shares in these companies are naturally riskier, because the stock price has no public track record for investors to judge by. You can find out more about IPOs in Chapters 3 and 4.

MUTUAL FUNDS

A *mutual fund* is a collection of similar investments. When you buy a share in a mutual fund, you are buying a percentage ownership of a big collection of stocks or bonds, but you are not buying any stocks or bonds directly. You can find out more about mutual funds in Chapter 6.

OTHER TYPES OF INVESTMENTS

Almost anything can be an investment if you think it will make money in the future—for example, a house, a painting, or certain types of insurance policies. You can find more about other investments in Chapter 8.

MATCH YOUR INVESTMENTS TO YOUR GOAL

While taking the long-term view is a good philosophy in general, sometimes you may have a short-term goal. In that case, you may want a different strategy.

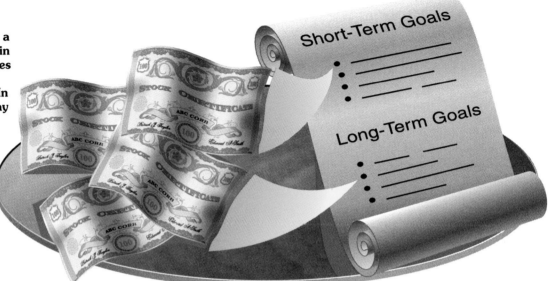

AN INVESTMENT SCHEDULE

The main idea is to have money available when you need it—a concept called *liquidity*. A secondary goal is to earn the highest returns possible for as long as possible.

For example, it does not do you much good to have your money in a high-interest-bearing bank certificate if you will need the cash before the certificate matures. It will probably cost you a steep penalty to take the money out early.

On the other hand, you are missing out on potential returns if you find yourself with a large balance in your checking account month after month. You apparently do not need to have that much cash available on a regular basis, and your checking account probably pays you little, if any, interest. That money could be earning higher interest, dividends, or appreciation in a different investment, even one that makes it difficult for you to get the money out.

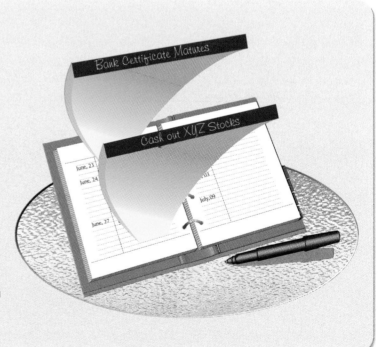

A CLOSER MATCH

If you want to fine-tune your investments even further, you can try to buy securities whose maturities match the date when you think you will need the money.

WHEN TO BUY

A basic rule is this: If you will need the money in three years or less, keep it liquid in a bank account, a money market fund that buys U.S. government securities, or maybe in the stock of a big, established company that pays dividends. The longer you can wait for the money, the better it is to buy stocks—especially the stocks of young, growing companies.

FIND A COMFORTABLE LEVEL OF RISK

The section "Match Your Investments to Your Goal" covers trying to synchronize the types of investments you choose with the time frame in which you will need money. The problem is that you may end up with investments that are right for your needs, but not your personality.

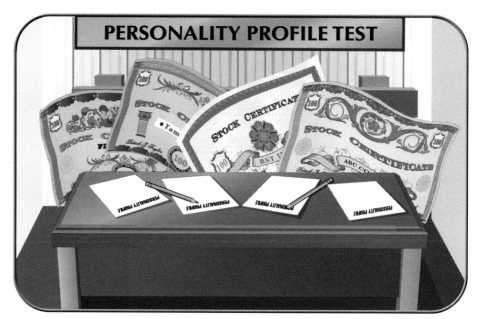

PERSONALITY PROFILE TEST

RE-EVALUATING YOUR GOALS AND TIMELINE

In the section "Set Your Financial Goals" earlier in this chapter, you set estimates of your financial goals. Whether your goal is saving for college, a vacation, a house, or something else, you have to answer three key questions:

- How much money will you need to achieve your goal?
- How much time do you have to reach your goal?
- How much money can you realistically set aside to invest toward your goal?

If the attempt to match investments with your time horizon produces a portfolio that makes you uncomfortable—for example, if it requires investments that are too risky for your taste—then you can try to change the answer to one or more of these three key questions.

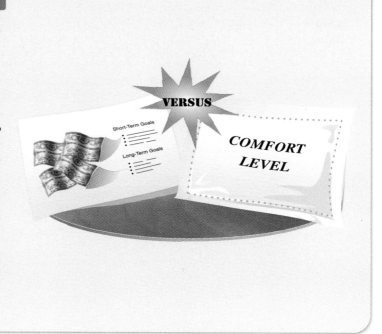

HOW MUCH RISK

If you have only a little money to invest and an expensive goal you are trying to reach, you will need your investments to produce a lot of money. To make matters even tougher, if you have only a short time to reach your goal, you will need to accumulate that money fast. That will require you to earn very high returns—which means taking on a high level of risk.

By contrast, if you need to earn a smaller amount, you can probably afford to reduce your risk and choose investments with lower returns.

The more money you can contribute, or the smaller your goal, or the longer your time frame, then the less risk you need to take.

Some people thrive on risk—they like to go mountain climbing, car-racing, or rafting in whitewater rivers. Others are extremely cautious. However, most people would prefer some combination of returns and safety.

EASING THE RISK

In order to shrink the risk level of the investments you will need, you will probably have to shrink your goal in some way.

You may decide to put off your goal for another year. Because that gives you more time in which to accumulate money, you can choose investments that build returns more slowly.

You may decide to scale down the size of your goal. That could mean buying a smaller house or living on a tighter budget in retirement. Then you will not need to amass as much money.

You may decide to curtail your standard of living now, using the extra money you will be saving to make a bigger contribution to your investments. Because you will be putting more money aside for your goal, you will not have to earn as much in returns.

A RISK QUIZ

How much risk are you comfortable with? Ask yourself these questions:

1. Which would make you more unhappy:
   a. If you owned a lot of stocks when the market was going down
   b. If you owned no stocks when the market was rising

2. What would you do if your stock holdings fell 50% in six months?
   a. Sell your holdings
   b. Buy more
   c. Hold onto what you have

Self-Evaluation:

If you answered (a) to both questions, you have a low tolerance for risk. You may want to adjust your goals and your investment mix accordingly.

If you answered (b) to both questions, you like a challenge. Go for a little risk!

If you answered a combination of (a), (b), or (c) to the questions, you are somewhere in between, comfortable with a moderate level of risk.

DETERMINE YOUR ASSET ALLOCATION

Choosing investments is a very personal decision, and you could well fashion a portfolio that is unlike anyone else's in the world. But here are some general suggestions for matching your risk tolerance.

A CONSERVATIVE PORTFOLIO

A person with low risk tolerance will have the least amount of stocks in his or her portfolio, because those are the riskiest of the standard investment categories. This person will be especially wary of young, untested companies and foreign stocks, which are more likely to face financial difficulties. So this investor may have 20 percent or even less of his money in stocks and 80 percent or more in bonds. All the stocks and bonds, moreover, will probably be from big, established U.S. companies or, in the case of bonds, from the U.S. Treasury—what is known as *blue chip* holdings.

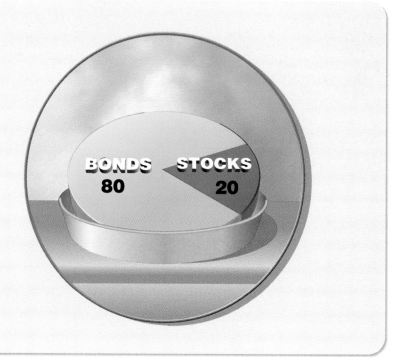

A MODERATE PORTFOLIO

A person who is willing to take some risk will have a portfolio more evenly matched between stocks and bonds, perhaps tilted a bit toward stocks. Among the stocks, this investor will also include a variety of types.

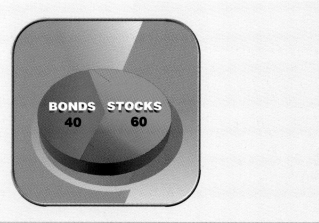

AN AGGRESSIVE PORTFOLIO

A person who is willing to take a chance on achieving high returns will have the most stocks, especially stocks of new companies, companies in high-growth industries, and companies outside the United States. The portfolio could well be 80 percent allocated to stocks. This person may also try other investments, such as IPOs, riskier bonds, and real estate.

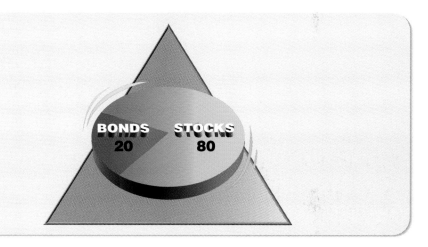

A STANDARD RULE

Your age also affects your investment strategy. In general, the older you are, the less risk you are usually willing to take. That is because, if you lose a lot of money, you do not have much time in which to earn it back.

Therefore, some experts follow the rule that you should have your age invested in bonds. That is, if you are 45 years old, then 45 percent of your holdings should be in bonds.

AVOID COMMON EMOTIONAL PITFALLS: DO YOU LOOK LIKE THIS?

Investing involves more than strategies and mathematical percentages. Often, you make decisions based on gut feelings, instinct, nervousness, hope, and a range of other emotions. That means you have to be careful not to fall into some common emotional traps.

For more trading advice, see Chapter 12.

OVERCONFIDENCE

Maybe the worst thing that can happen to an investor is to actually make one great stock pick. Why? That person may start thinking that he or she is a genius at choosing stocks. The next thing you know, the investor may risk large sums of money on hunches rather than solid research, thinking that the hunches of such a genius are sure to pay off.

DESPERATION

If you just lost a lot of money on an investment, you may start to panic and feel desperate to make up the loss. That can lead you to throw your money into overly risky investments without doing enough research.

EMOTIONAL INVOLVEMENT

You may have bought a stock because you truly believe in the company. You avidly read every word about it in the newspaper. When you are so committed to a company, it can be hard to give up your dream, even if the company is making serious mistakes and the stock is dropping badly.

IMPATIENCE

Some people, when they are stuck in heavy traffic, hop constantly from one lane to another, trying to find the fastest lane. Inevitably, as soon as they leave a lane, it speeds up.

Sometimes stock trading is like that. As soon as you sell a stock, it goes up, and the stock you just bought drops. It feels as if you can never win. But you certainly lose: Every time you buy or sell a stock, you pay a trading commission.

CHAPTER 3

Choosing an Online Broker

Can you get advice from your online brokers? How fast can they execute your trades? This chapter helps you decide what qualities are most important in selecting a broker—including cost, speed, size, and the types of services available.

COMPARE VARIOUS TYPES OF BROKERS

You can trade stocks, bonds, and mutual funds through dozens of different online sites—big and small brokerages, discount and full-service firms, old Wall Street names and new companies that exist only in cyberspace. This section shows you some sites that illustrate the range available.

COMPARE VARIOUS TYPES OF BROKERS

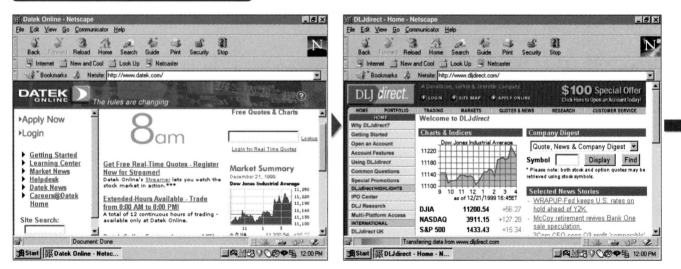

■ Datek Online's home page, www.datek.com. Datek is an example of a discount brokerage.

■ DLJdirect's home page, www.dljdirect.com. DLJdirect is an example of a full-service brokerage.

54

What are some of the major differences among all these sites?

Generally, online firms fall into one of two camps: *discount brokerages,* where you pay a low fee and get trading and not much else, and *full-service brokerages,* where you pay a lot more and get a lot more service—most notably advice.

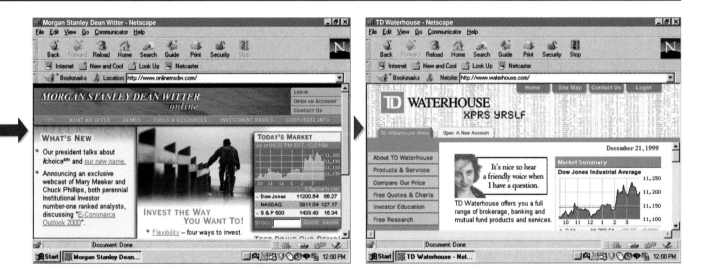

■ Morgan Stanley Dean Witter Online's home page, www.onlinemsdw.com. Morgan Stanley Dean Witter Online is an example of a full-service brokerage.

■ TD Waterhouse's home page, www.waterhouse.com. TD Waterhouse is an example of a medium-service brokerage, in between discount and full service.

CONSIDER YOUR BROKER'S RELIABILITY

First and foremost: If you are going to entrust your money to a brokerage site, you have to be able to count on it to do what you ask with minimal technological glitches.

OVERLOAD

Unfortunately, some online brokerages have had trouble coping if a lot of people want to trade at once.

For instance, in November 1998, when theglobe.com (a company that allows users to create personalized Web pages) sold stock publicly for the first time, demand was so heavy that orders piled up at some brokerages. As the price doubled and tripled and eventually shot up to more than ten times the opening price of $9, many investors frantically tried to cancel earlier buy orders.

Charles Schwab Corp. had to settle complaints from 300 clients whose cancellations got lost in a backlog.

COMPUTER BREAKDOWNS

Even the largest companies with the newest technology are not safe from computer crashes.

In a survey of big online brokerages by *The Wall Street Journal* in the fall of 1999, all eight firms that responded reported suffering computer outages lasting at least half an hour—and some as long as four or five hours. Several companies had multiple breakdowns within the year.

E*Trade has been sued by investors over a series of breakdowns. An arbitration panel awarded one customer more than $9,000.

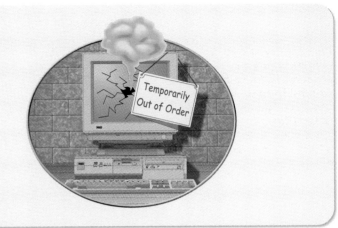

WHAT CAN CAUSE A BREAKDOWN?

Computer outages can result from a number of factors. For example, debugging or upgrading one system can unintentionally wreak havoc on a connected system. Problems may also lie in an outside program that the brokerage uses rather than the brokerage's software itself.

CHECKING THE RECORD

With so many possible hazards, you need to check out the track record of a brokerage site before you choose to invest with it. You may want to start with *The Wall Street Journal* survey. Another good source is surveys by consumer magazines. For example, *Smart Money's* Web site (www.smartmoney.com) posts a survey that's updated every six months or so that looks at leading brokerages' computer downtimes, among other factors. When I checked in February 2000, Brown & Co. and Muriel Siebert had the best reliability ratings, and Datek had the worst.

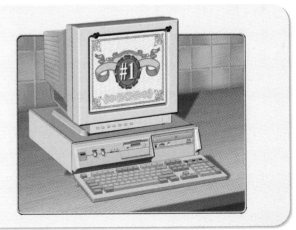

Chapter 11 offers some suggestions on how to protect yourself in case of technological trouble at your brokerage.

CALCULATE WHAT YOUR BROKER CHARGES

How much does it cost to buy one share of stock online? It depends on what you are paying for.

HOW TO PAY

Generally, you pay a fee for each trade you make. However, at some larger firms, you may have the option of choosing a very different method—paying a flat annual fee, based on the amount of assets in your account, for unlimited trades and personal advice.

WHICH PAYMENT METHOD IS BETTER?

Paying per-trade is preferable if you plan to do your own research and the only thing you want a brokerage to do is execute the trade. You should also pay this way if you do not plan to trade very much.

But if you expect to talk a lot with a broker, you are probably better off paying a fixed annual charge.

$29.95
$14.95
$9.95
$0.00

WHAT YOU PAY

PAYING PER TRADE

Here are some typical per-trade charges—generally for trading up to 1,000 shares—from a range of brokers:

Ameritrade	$ 8.00
Datek	$ 9.99
TD Waterhouse	$12.00
E*Trade	$14.95
Fidelity PowerStreet	$14.95
DLJdirect	$20.00
Accutrade	$29.95
Morgan Stanley Dean Witter Online	$29.95
Charles Schwab	$29.95
Merrill Lynch	$29.95

PAYING FOR EXTRAS

Per-trade fees are just the basic rates. If you trade more than 1,000 or 5,000 shares, plan to pay 2 cents to 3 cents per share instead for the entire order in most cases. Then you may be hit with other charges for the following:

- Trading fewer than 12 times a year
- Limit orders, which set a ceiling on the amount you will pay for a stock
- Stocks that do not trade on a major exchange
- Stocks that trade for under $1 per share

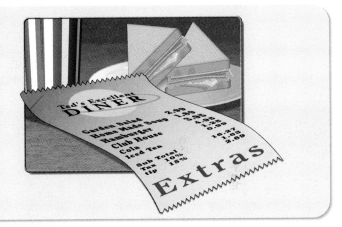

PAYING A FLAT ANNUAL FEE

Full-service brokerages, such as Merrill Lynch and Morgan Stanley Dean Witter, have various arrangements for their annual fees. The charges run around 0.5 percent to 2 percent of the assets you have invested with the company. But it depends on just how much you have, how much advice you want from your broker, and the types of investments you make.

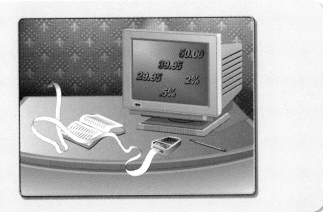

No one can trade in a vacuum. Even at the discount brokerages, you can expect a few basic perks, such as instant price quotes on any stock you want and important news updates about the market. Bigger, more expensive sites offer you many more services.

MARKET RESEARCH

If you trade through a major Wall Street firm, you should get reports on stocks and bonds from the research staff and maybe recommendations alerting you to their favorite picks.

Other common offerings include links to news services like Reuters and third-party research like Zacks Investment Research's summary of analysts' forecasts.

AFTER-HOURS TRADING

While the markets may close at 4:00 p.m., the Internet doesn't have business hours. So most firms let you trade before the markets officially open or after they close—or both. However, be warned that you will probably pay a higher price for trading after-hours. Because there are fewer other buyers and sellers at these times, you won't get as wide a range of bids and offers.

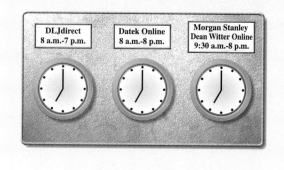

| DLJdirect 8 a.m.-7 p.m. | Datek Online 8 a.m.-8 p.m. | Morgan Stanley Dean Witter Online 9:30 a.m.-8 p.m. |

A SHOT AT INITIAL PUBLIC OFFERINGS

Initial public offerings, known as *IPOs*, mark a company's first-ever sale of stock to the public. And with some issues zooming up 70 percent or even 100 percent on their opening day, more and more online investors want a crack at them.

This is where the big brokerages have a strong advantage. Because other departments of these firms may be involved in the actual stock offering, brokers can reserve shares for Web site clients before outside firms get a chance. So a number of brokerages—including Charles Schwab, Ameritrade Holding Corp., TD Waterhouse, and National Discount Brokers, Inc.—are trying to set up ties with investment banks to give their clients similar access.

But not everyone is enthralled with these investments. Just as fast as they rise, they can also crash. So some brokers limit online purchases of IPOs until the second day of trading.

SOMEONE TO TALK TO

No matter how savvy an investor you are, you may have questions about how to use a Web site or how to cope with computer problems. Don't worry—you won't be left dangling in cyberspace. Even the lowest-frill, lowest-fee brokerage sites have real, live customer service personnel available by phone 24 hours a day. A few brokerage sites also have branch offices you can visit, such as Charles Schwab, Merrill Lynch, Morgan Stanley Dean Witter, and TD Waterhouse.

AFTER YOU BUY YOUR STOCK . . .

The big brokerages can link your online trading account to other services. You can set up an individual retirement account (IRA), figure out how to save for college, or get advice regarding tax-planning strategies.

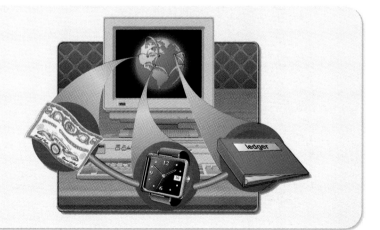

CHECK OUT SAMPLE BROKERS' SERVICES

Each Web brokerage has a menu of products and services that is as unique as its home page.

INVESTMENT SERVICES

Discount Fees

Long Trading Hours

Real-time Balances

Bond Trading

Real-time Quotes

CHECK OUT SAMPLE BROKERS' SERVICES

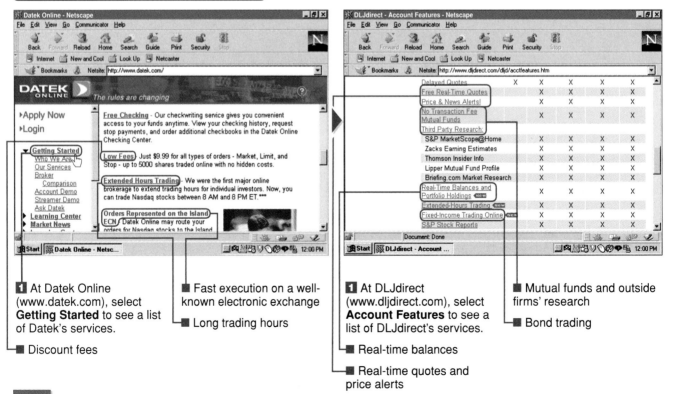

1 At Datek Online (www.datek.com), select **Getting Started** to see a list of Datek's services.

■ Discount fees

■ Fast execution on a well-known electronic exchange

■ Long trading hours

1 At DLJdirect (www.dljdirect.com), select **Account Features** to see a list of DLJdirect's services.

■ Real-time balances

■ Real-time quotes and price alerts

■ Mutual funds and outside firms' research

■ Bond trading

Can I get some of these services without using a broker?

You can get the services that come from outside vendors—for example, news from the Reuters wire or mutual fund profiles from Lipper Analytical Services.

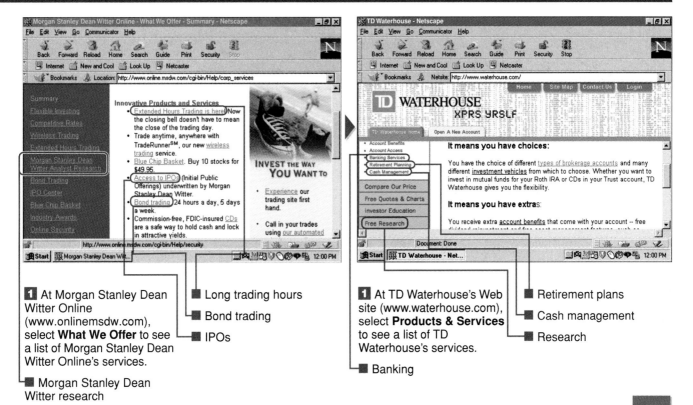

1 At Morgan Stanley Dean Witter Online (www.onlinemsdw.com), select **What We Offer** to see a list of Morgan Stanley Dean Witter Online's services.

■ Morgan Stanley Dean Witter research

■ Long trading hours

■ Bond trading

■ IPOs

1 At TD Waterhouse's Web site (www.waterhouse.com), select **Products & Services** to see a list of TD Waterhouse's services.

■ Banking

■ Retirement plans

■ Cash management

■ Research

COMPARE BROKERS' SPEEDS

Fast trading is one of the major reasons people choose to invest online. So the last thing an investor needs is a pokey brokerage that takes forever to finish a trade.

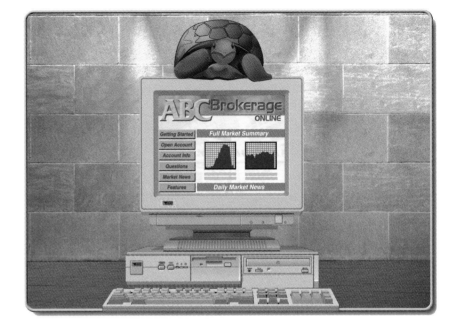

HOW SLOW IS TOO SLOW?

Your broker is too slow if he takes so long to execute your trade that other investors jump in ahead of you, pushing up the price.

Chapter 11 discusses some more ramifications of trading speed.

TESTING BROKERAGE SITES

Try this test: Without signing up as a customer, log on to a brokerage site and see how fast its pages load. Maneuver from page to page. Use the site's trading simulation, if it has one.

WHO IS THE FASTEST OF THEM ALL?

A company called Keynote Systems, Inc., measures the average response time of 40 consumer Web sites—including 10 brokerages—by downloading them for 16 hours every day. You can find out which brokerages ranked best over the most recent eight weeks by going to Keynote's Web site, www.keynote.com—which, yes, downloads itself pretty fast.

When I checked, Charles Schwab, Web Street, and DLJdirect were on top, with Bull & Bear, Brown & Co., and Morgan Stanley Dean Witter Online way at the bottom. The speediest sites took around 12 to 14 seconds to get a stock quote and acknowledge an order to buy a stock.

WHOSE FAULT IS IT?

Before you curse your broker for being slow, make sure your problem was not caused by your own computer, modem speed, or Internet service provider. You can do that by trying other Web sites and comparing how fast they load to how fast your broker's site loads. Another test: Try logging off and logging back on to the Internet.

If you like chat rooms, go on in and ask if anyone has had problems with the site you are checking.

COMPARE BROKERS' PERKS

Competition on the Internet is so fierce that brokers are offering all sorts of inducements to draw in new customers— just the way banks used to give away toasters and gas stations handed out glassware.

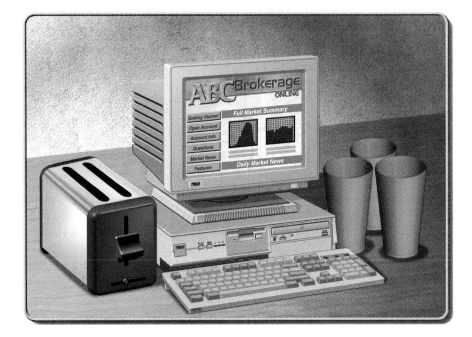

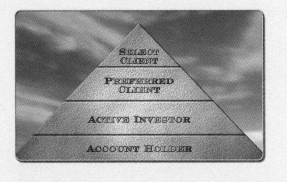

TYPES OF PERKS

EXOTIC VACATIONS

Online brokerages have been known to dole out trips to Hawaii, London, Mexico, and the Super Bowl. Usually it is for new accounts, but E*Trade's Super Bowl XXXIV offer was a lottery, open to anyone.

DISCOUNTED COMMISSIONS

Typically, investors can pay lower commissions if they keep at least $100,000 in their accounts or make a minimum number of trades. The minimum varies widely from brokerage to brokerage—from 30 trades a year to 30 trades a quarter (or more).

In November 1999, American Express Co. went one better: Anyone with just $25,000 in assets could buy stocks online for free.

SIGN-UP BONUSES

E*Trade and Fidelity have given a $100 bonus to people who open a new account. Ameritrade rebated half of all first-month commissions for anyone who became a client in the first two months of 2000. Sign up at Schwab's site, and you could get a $25 gift certificate at online bookseller Amazon.com.

Some brokers even promise cash to anyone who deserts a rival site!

SPECIAL INVESTMENTS

For their very best customers, online brokerages reserve investment opportunities not open to just anyone—including certain initial public offerings, private equity deals, and the firms' own mutual funds.

CONSIDER THE SIZE OF THE BROKERAGE

Does size matter? Well, big brokerages and smaller ones definitely have some differences.

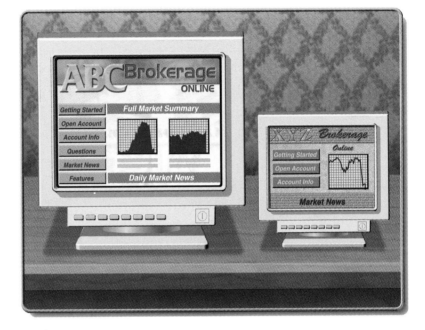

FINANCIAL BACKING

You want to make sure that your broker has the money to cover you in case of a major disaster. One common concern: A broker could let high-risk day traders borrow too much on *margin*, or credit. If the traders lose badly, so could the broker.

Of course, all brokerages are required by law to keep customer assets segregated from their own. This means that if you own 100 shares of Microsoft today, and tomorrow a hurricane rips apart your broker's office—or the stock market crashes 1,000 points—you still own 100 shares of Microsoft. But the more financial backing behind a brokerage, the better it will be able to weather such catastrophes.

PRODUCTS AND PRICE

The larger the firm, the more services it is likely to provide. These services can include original research, financial planning tools, and the ability to get in on initial public offerings.

Of course, the biggest firms also tend to be the most expensive.

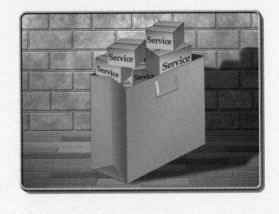

MATCH YOUR OBJECTIVES TO YOUR BROKER

With so many brokerages, each offering such a wide and different array of features, how can you possibly choose? How can you even compare them?

SETTING YOUR PRIORITIES

You should not pay for something you do not need. So the first thing you have to do is decide which services are most important to you:

- Do you plan to trade often? If not, the cost per trade will not matter much.

- Do you intend to do your own research? You need research tools like company reports and access to news sites.

- Do you want to invest in IPOs and private placements? If so, you should consider and compare the minimums that brokers require you to keep in your account in order to gain access to these investments.

Do you plan to trade often? ✓

Do you intend to do your own research? ✓

Do you want to invest in IPOs and private placements?

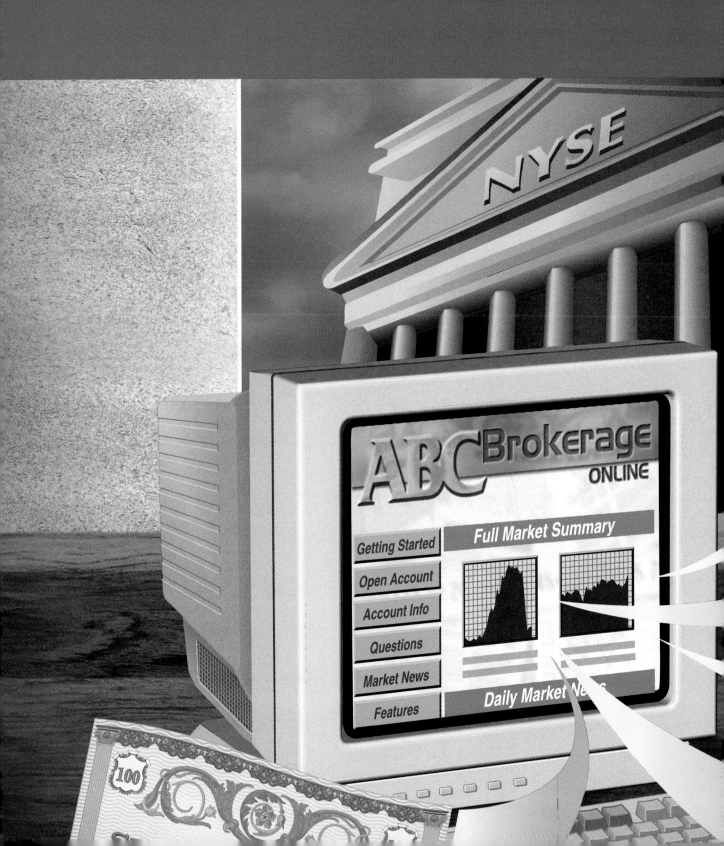

CHAPTER 4

Trading Stocks Online

What kinds of stocks are the riskiest? Which are safer? Do you have to be a millionaire to open an online account? This chapter shows you how to trade stocks online and explains stock terms, such as P/E and dividend yield.

UNDERSTAND HOW THE STOCK MARKET WORKS

When you buy a share of stock, you buy a small percentage of the company that issued the stock. You are now one of the owners of the company.

HOW SHARES ARE ISSUED

Imagine a company that is founded and completely owned by one person. Its only source of capital is its profits plus whatever that owner puts in from his own pocket.

In order to raise more money, the owner decides to bring in additional owners. He divides the total value of the company into ten equal parts, or *shares*. Then he sells eight of the shares to other people, keeping two for himself. Now the company can also spend the money these eight investors paid for their shares.

Now the company has ten owners, or *shareholders*. These shareholders can either keep their shares or sell them to other investors.

STOCK EXCHANGES VERSUS NETWORKS

In a traditional auction exchange, each stock has a *specialist*—a firm that takes every order to buy or sell and finds a match on the other end. That's pretty much the way the New York Stock Exchange has been trading stocks since 1792.

Alternatively, you can trade stocks "over the counter," without specialists. *Over the counter* simply means that brokers take orders to buy or sell stocks and post them on the NASDAQ exchange for other brokers to match.

And now, investors can trade directly with each other on the Internet. Electronic communications networks, or *ECNs*, display buy and sell orders online.

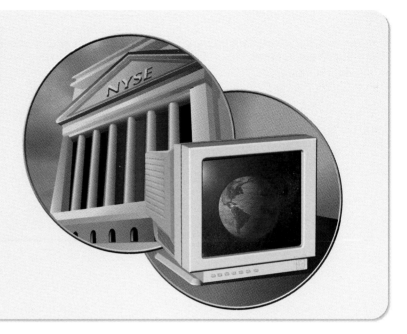

TWO WAYS TO MAKE MONEY

The main way to profit from a stock is to sell it—eventually—for a higher price than you paid. Your profit is called *capital gains*. Studies have shown that, since 1925, the typical big-company stock has gained an average of 11 percent per year.

In addition, you may pick up some extra cash if the company you invest in pays a dividend. A *dividend* is a small percentage of earnings that some companies distribute quarterly to shareholders, allocated as "so many cents per share." For example, Ford and GM pay 50 cents per share quarterly, whereas Disney pays about 5 cents.

DISTINGUISH BETWEEN DIFFERENT TYPES OF STOCKS

How do you pick among the approximately 8,000 different stocks that are publicly traded in the United States? Start by classifying them according to their size and their level of risk.

CHOOSING SMALL, MEDIUM, OR LARGE

Market capitalization—often abbreviated *market cap*—refers to the total value of all of a company's shares. Typically, companies are labeled small-cap, medium-cap, or large-cap.

SIZING UP THE DOLLARS: A CHANGING DEFINITION

But what is small and what is large? The definition of *small* keeps inching upward as the stock market rises.

Still, you can probably assume that small-cap stocks have a market capitalization of less than $1 billion, medium-cap stocks—$1 billion to $5 billion, and large-cap stocks—more than $5 billion.

In general, smaller companies are considered riskier.

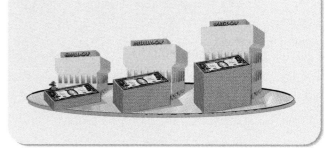

CLASSIFYING STOCKS BY RISK

LOW RISK: VALUE STOCKS

People who buy *value stocks* are bargain hunters: They believe that the stock's price is low—or *undervalued*—compared with the company's fundamentals. Value stocks' prices tend to drop less over time than other types. But if their investors are right, they should rise more.

Big, established companies in stable industries are most likely to be found in the value stock grouping. These companies also tend to pay dividends.

The top ten holdings in Vanguard Group's Value Index fund include Exxon Mobil Corp. (oil), Citigroup, Inc. (financial services), American International Group, Inc. (insurance), and AT&T Corp. (telecommunications).

MODERATE RISK: GROWTH STOCKS

The defining characteristic of *growth stocks* is a steady pattern of earnings growth. In practice, this means that they are typically companies that are newer, smaller, and faster-growing than value stocks, but still established enough to have a track record. Often, they dominate their industries. The growth stock category is where you can put the bigger and older technology companies.

The top ten holdings in Vanguard Group's U.S. Growth fund include Cisco Systems, Inc. (technology), Microsoft Corp. (technology), General Electric Co. (electricity/diversified), and Lucent Technologies, Inc. (technology).

HIGH RISK: EMERGING GROWTH STOCKS

The newest, fastest-growing—and riskiest—are *emerging* or *aggressive growth stocks.* These may be Internet startups, for instance.

At the end of 1999, the top ten holdings of Vanguard's Aggressive Growth Fund included CMGI, Inc. (Internet investments), Computer Sciences Corp. (information technology services), MedImmune, Inc. (biotech), and LAM Research Corp. (semiconductor processing equipment). (Remember that by their very nature, these stocks are volatile, so their status may change from emerging growth stocks to ordinary growth stocks—or they could even crash—by the time you read this.)

OWNING VERSUS MANAGING

So you own a
share of stock. But
do you really own
the company?

PROFESSIONAL MANAGERS

Even though shareholders are the official owners,
they do not run a company the way the owner of a
small business does. They are more like silent
partners. The company hires a *chief executive
officer* (CEO) and other professional managers to
oversee day-to-day operations.

THE OWNERS' POWER

Theoretically, shareholders make important decisions
for their company when they vote on resolutions at
their annual meeting. As a practical matter, most
shareholders either do not vote or just vote the way
management recommends.

Now and then, however, when profits are particularly
low or passions are particularly high, activist
shareholders have managed to rally the votes to push
through significant changes. They have forced out
weak managements and persuaded companies to stop
using child labor in developing countries, for example.

Over time, the stock market in general will rise, but this does not mean that *every* stock will do well. Some will gain more than the overall market average, and some less.

If you could predict just which stocks will soar, you could make a lot of money by buying them early. That is called *outperforming,* or *beating,* the market.

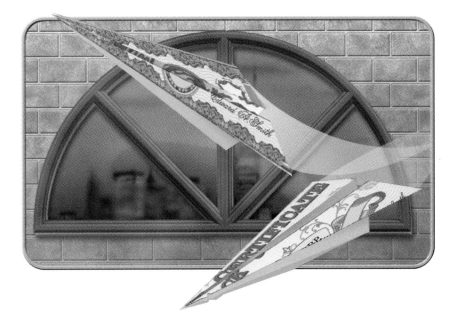

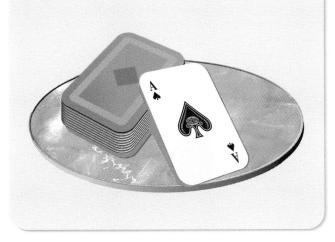

ACTIVE INVESTING

The search for better-than-average stocks is called *active investing*. Professional managers are paid high salaries to pick out superstar stocks.

However, coming up with winners consistently isn't easy.

INVESTING IN INDEX FUNDS

Many experts say that you should simply ride along with the market and not try to select too many particular stocks.

To do that, you can invest in an *index fund*—a mutual fund that chooses a collection of stocks to mirror one of the indexes, or yardsticks, that is used to track the direction of the entire market. You can find out more about mutual funds in Chapter 6.

You may still want to set aside a little money for your own stock-picking—just in case you find that winner.

FIND OUT A STOCK PRICE

On many Web sites—portals like Yahoo! and Excite, news sites, and special financial sites—you can look up a stock price almost instantaneously. This chapter uses Quicken.com as an example, but all the price finders work pretty much the same.

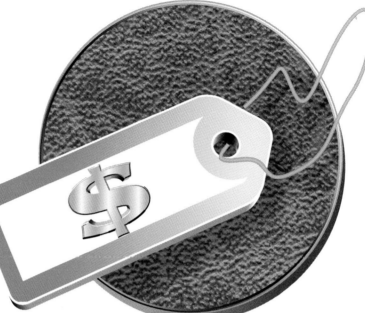

FIND A STOCK'S PRICE IF YOU KNOW ITS TICKER SYMBOL

1 At Quicken.com (www.quicken.com), enter the stock's ticker symbol.

2 Click **Go**.

■ **Last Trade** shows the price the stock traded at most recently.

■ **Change** shows how much the price has risen or fallen since the close of the previous day.

How up-to-the-minute is the price?
There is typically a 15- to 20-minute time lag.

FIND A STOCK'S PRICE IF YOU DON'T KNOW ITS TICKER SYMBOL

1 At Quicken.com (www.quicken.com), click **Don't Know the Symbol**?

2 Click the circle next to **Stock**.

3 Enter as much of the company's name you know.

4 Click **Search**.

■ Quicken.com returns a list of companies that could match the partial name you entered and their ticker symbols.

5 Click **Quote** next to the company's name to see its stock price.

GET SOME BASIC INFORMATION ABOUT A COMPANY

Before you put your money at risk buying shares, you should do some research into the company, its financial condition, its past, and its prospects. You can find this kind of information at several investing sites; this chapter uses Quicken.com and 411Stocks as examples.

GET COMPANY INFORMATION FROM QUICKEN.COM

1 Follow the steps in the section "Finding Out a Stock Price" to get to a stock's information page.

2 Click **Fundamentals**.

■ The value of all the shares combined.

■ Which exchange the stock trades on.

■ How many shares have traded that day. You probably want a stock with fairly large volume, because you can more easily find buyers and sellers.

■ This page gives a historical perspective on the company and its peers, showing how its income, revenue, and earnings per share have grown over the past 10 years compared with the average for its industry.

Note: In this particular case, the numbers indicate that Cisco is generally outperforming its industry.

3 Scroll down for more information.

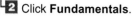

How can I learn more about a company?

Most companies have their own Web sites. Usually, the URL is www.companyname.com, where companyname is the company's name.

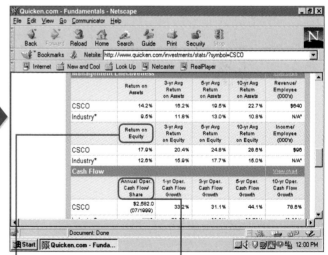

www.companyname.com

■ The dividend payment divided by the current stock price. That results in a percentage, which you can compare to the interest rate you may receive on a bank account. Cisco pays no dividend, so the yield is zero.

■ Total debt divided by total market cap. A high ratio would mean the company is pinched for cash.

4 Scroll down for more information.

■ Essentially, this is profit divided by equity – in other words, how much you are earning for each share you own. You can compare this percentage to the returns from other types of investments.

■ If cash flow is too low, a company may have to borrow or issue more stock to raise money, both of which could hurt the value of your shares. **CONTINUED**

GET SOME BASIC INFORMATION
ABOUT A COMPANY (CONTINUED)

You should put all your research on returns, income growth, cash flow, and everything else in perspective. Compare the company's performance to the rest of its industry, and compare the returns to those of other investments.

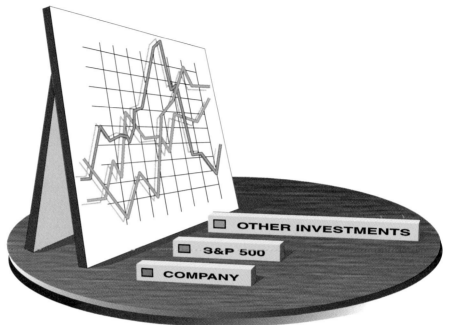

OTHER INVESTMENTS

S&P 500

COMPANY

GET COMPANY INFORMATION FROM 411STOCKS

1 At 411Stocks (www.411stocks.com), enter the ticker symbol.

2 Click **Get**.

■ Net earnings divided by the number of shares. This should consistently increase.

■ A large difference between today's high and low could indicate a bumpy ride for shareholders.

■ Price-earnings ratio, or how much investors are willing to pay for each $1 of the company's earnings. Anything above 25 is a sign of investor confidence.

3 Scroll down for more information.

Which are the most important numbers regarding a stock?

Most people focus on P/E ratio and the current stock price. But even more important is whether the numbers are moving up or down.

411Stocks' Data Sheet for CSCO - Netscape

File Edit View Go Communicator Help

Back Forward Reload Home Search Guide Print Security Stop

Bookmarks Location: http://411stocks.stockselector.com/stocks.asp?symbol=csco

Internet New and Cool Look Up Netcaster RealPlayer

Price Data

Today's Volume:	5,363,200	Last Tick:	EVEN
Today's High:	107.19	52 Week High:	107.00
Today's Low:	105.94	52 Week Low:	44.94

Basic Fundamental Data

PE Ratio:	177.00	Estimated Growth Rate:	29.03%
Earnings/Share:	$0.60	PEG Ratio:	6.10
Dividend/Share:	N/A	Shares Outstanding:	3,421.2 Mil
Yield:	N/A	Market Cap:	$366.5 Bil
Book Value:	$4.06	Revenue/Share:	$3.93
Price/Book Value:	26.39	Price/Sales:	27.26
% Owned by Insiders:	2.3%	% Held by Institutions:	62.8%

Technical Data

25 Day Average:	$99.30	MACD:	2.23
200 Day Average:	$67.59	Beta:	1.47

Connect: Contacting host: m.doubleclick.net...

Start | 411Stocks' Data Sheet for... | 12:00 PM

411Stocks' Data Sheet for CSCO - Netscape

File Edit View Go Communicator Help

Back Forward Reload Home Search Guide Print Security Stop

Bookmarks Location: http://411stocks.stockselector.com/stocks.asp?symbol=csco

Internet New and Cool Look Up Netcaster RealPlayer

Copyright (c) 1999, StockSelector.com, All Rights Reserved

Financial Ratios

Profit Margin:	15.00%	Return on Assets:	11.60%
Return on Equity:	14.50%	Return on Investment:	N/A
Current Ratio:	1.5%	Quick Ratio:	1.3%
Cash Ratio:	0.9%	Debt to Equity:	0.0%
Inventory Turnover:	8.0%	Receivables Turnover:	9.1%

Balance Sheet (millions)

Cash & Equivalents:	$1,251.0	Short-term Debt:	$0.0
Fixed Assets:	$898.0	Other Liabilities:	$496.0
Intangibles:	$0.0	Total Liabilities:	$3,525.0
Other Assets:	$15,258.0	Total Equity:	$13,882.0
Total Assets:	$17,407.0	Total Liabilities & Equity:	$17,407.0

Income Statement (millions)

Connect: Host m.doubleclick.net contacted. Waiting for reply...

Start | 411Stocks' Data She... | 12:00 PM

■ How much shareholders would receive if all the company's tangible assets were sold off. Book value is a traditional way of gauging financial strength, but it has become less popular for technology companies.

■ The most common way of measuring risk. Cisco's beta of 1.47 means that, on average, it moves 1.47 percent each time the market as a whole moves 1 percent.

■ Total number of shares.

4 Scroll down to see this financial ratio and balance sheet information.

SEE HOW A STOCK HAS PERFORMED OVER TIME

Today's stock price tells you only about today. To get a more complete picture, you need to go to the site where you got the price and call up a chart showing the stock's performance over at least the past year.

SEE HOW A STOCK HAS PERFORMED OVER TIME

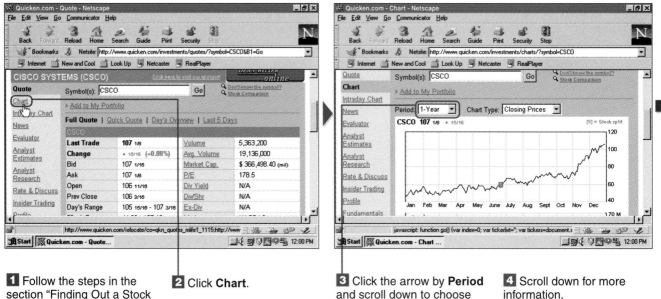

1 Follow the steps in the section "Finding Out a Stock Price" to get to a stock information page like this one.

2 Click **Chart**.

3 Click the arrow by **Period** and scroll down to choose the time period you want (from one day to five years).

4 Scroll down for more information.

? **Which index should I use for comparison?**

Generally, you should compare large companies to the Standard & Poor's 500 and small or high-tech companies to the NASDAQ.

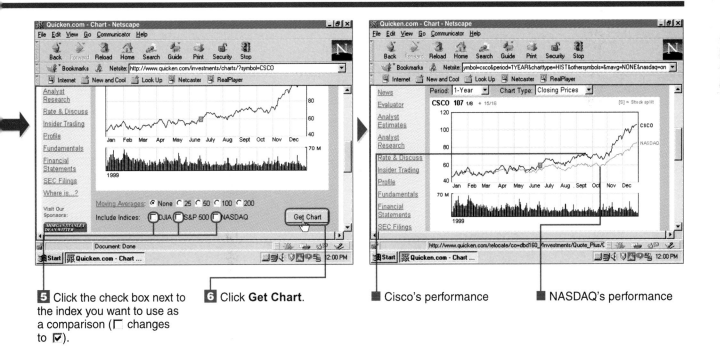

5 Click the check box next to the index you want to use as a comparison (☐ changes to ☑).

6 Click **Get Chart**.

■ Cisco's performance

■ NASDAQ's performance

DISCOVER WHAT THE EXPERTS THINK ABOUT A STOCK

The job of a professional analyst is to research the stocks in a particular industry. Microsoft Corp.'s MSN MoneyCentral Investor (moneycentral.msn.com) and BigCharts (www.bigcharts.com) look at these analysts' findings in two different ways.

CHECK OUT ANALYSTS' REPORTS WITH MONEYCENTRAL INVESTOR

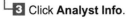

1 At MoneyCentral (moneycentral.msn.com), enter the ticker symbol of the stock you want information about.

2 Click **Go**.

3 Click **Analyst Info**.

■ This page shows the range of earnings estimates.

4 Click **Ratings** to see the analysts' buy and sell recommendations.

Should I trust what the analysts say?

They are professionals who know their industry. But they tend to be overly bullish.

CHECK OUT ANALYSTS' REPORTS WITH BIGCHARTS

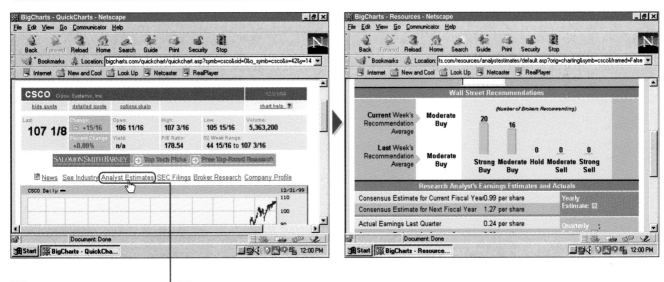

1 At BigCharts (www.bigcharts.com), enter the ticker symbol of the stock you want information about.

2 Click **Quick Chart**.

3 Click **Analyst Estimates**.

■ This page shows whether analysts recommend buying the stock.

FIND OUT ABOUT A COMPANY'S FINANCES BY CHECKING ITS GOVERNMENT DOCUMENTS

One of the best places to do your research on a company is the U.S. Securities and Exchange Commission's online database, EDGAR, at www.sec.gov. EDGAR is a treasure trove of data, with all the important financial filings from most companies.

FIND ABOUT A COMPANY'S FINANCES BY CHECKING ITS GOVERNMENT DOCUMENTS

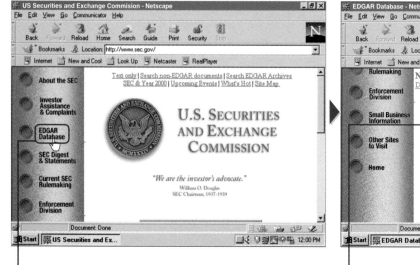

1 At the U.S. Securities and Exchange Commission's Web site (www.sec.gov), click **EDGAR Database**.

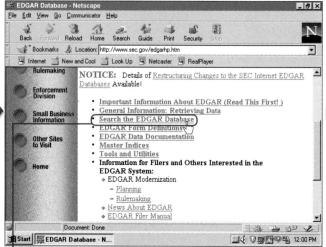

2 Click **Search the EDGAR Database**.

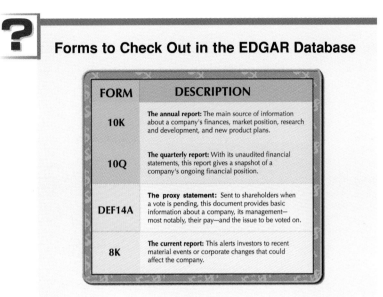

Forms to Check Out in the EDGAR Database

FORM	DESCRIPTION
10K	**The annual report:** The main source of information about a company's finances, market position, research and development, and new product plans.
10Q	**The quarterly report:** With its unaudited financial statements, this report gives a snapshot of a company's ongoing financial position.
DEF14A	**The proxy statement:** Sent to shareholders when a vote is pending, this document provides basic information about a company, its management—most notably, their pay—and the issue to be voted on.
8K	**The current report:** This alerts investors to recent material events or corporate changes that could affect the company.

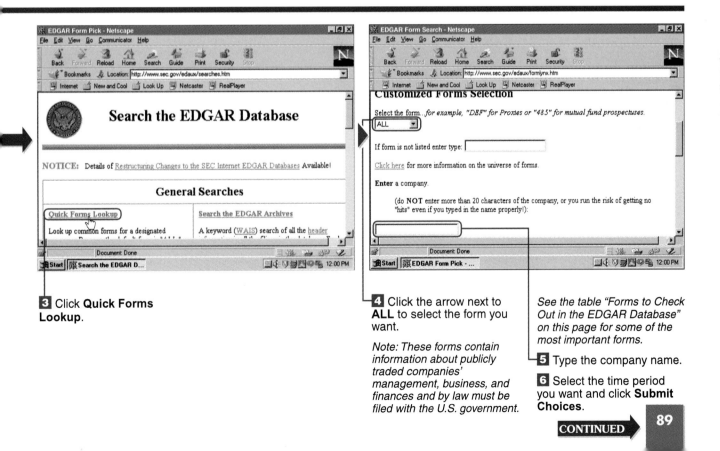

3 Click **Quick Forms Lookup**.

4 Click the arrow next to **ALL** to select the form you want.

Note: These forms contain information about publicly traded companies' management, business, and finances and by law must be filed with the U.S. government.

See the table "Forms to Check Out in the EDGAR Database" on this page for some of the most important forms.

5 Type the company name.

6 Select the time period you want and click **Submit Choices**.

CONTINUED

To give one example of the SEC's treasures: From a company's proxy statement, you can find out the names of all the top executives and how much they are paid.

FINANCIAL FILES

7 Click the company name next to the form you want.

Note: You probably want the most recent filing.

■ This section of the DEF 14A form shows you the salary and bonuses for the chief executive officer, executive vice president, and senior vice president for the past three years.

Note: The documents are very long, but the key information is fairly easy to find within all that verbiage.

Do all companies that issue stock file these reports on EDGAR?

All except the very smallest public U.S. companies are required by law to file these reports. However, foreign companies—even if they trade on U.S. exchanges—are exempt from most online filing requirements.

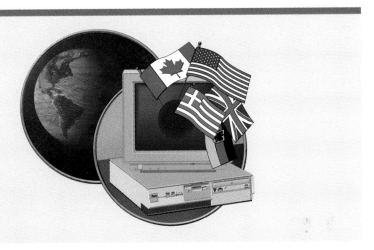

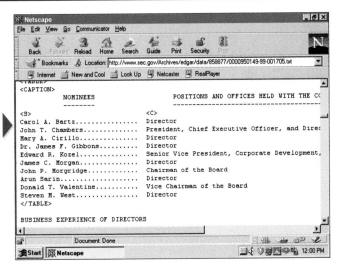

■ This section of the DEF 14A form shows you the stock options for top executives.

■ This section of the DEF 14A form shows you the nominees for the Board of Directors.

8 Scroll down for brief biographical sketches of each nominee.

Note: You should check to see if there are too many company officials or people with close connections to top executives.

CATCH UP WITH THE NEWS ABOUT THE MARKETS

A company's business prospects—and therefore its stock price—are influenced by all sorts of events. You can track the headlines on a number of Web sites that specialize in finance and financial news.

THESTREET.COM

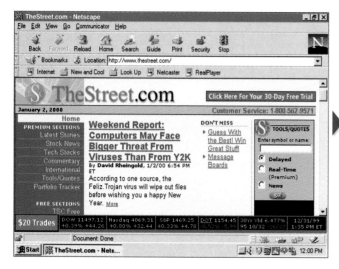

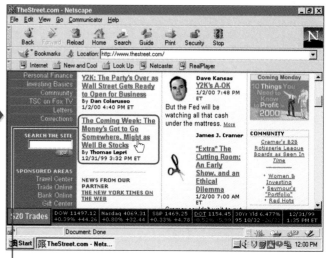

■ At TheStreet.com (www.thestreet.com), unlike most news sites, financial articles on the main site are available without charge, but subscribers have to pay to see additional commentary.

1 Scroll down for more headlines.

2 Click any headline to get the full story.

Where else can I get news online?

Most big newspapers and magazines have Web sites. Portals like Yahoo! and Excite also display headline news.

CBS MARKETWATCH

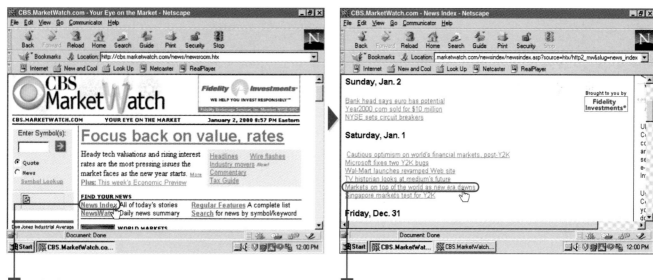

1 At CBS MarketWatch (cbs.marketwatch.com/), click **News Index** for headlines.

2 Click any headline to call up the full story.

CONTINUED ▶

Besides headlines and stories, you can get a range of investment services on many of these news sites—for example, stock prices and financial planning advice.

BLOOMBERG.COM

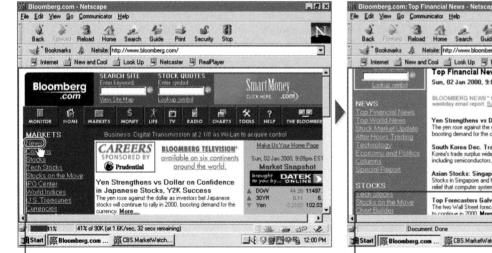

1 At Bloomberg.com (www.bloomberg.com), click **News**.

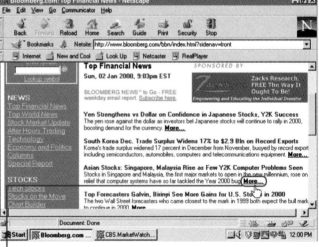

2 Click **More** for more information on any story.

?

What kinds of news should I read?

You certainly want anything about the company in which you own stock, its rivals, and its industry. Then you should take a look at more general stories about major developments affecting the countries where your company operates or gets raw materials from.

MONEYCENTRAL

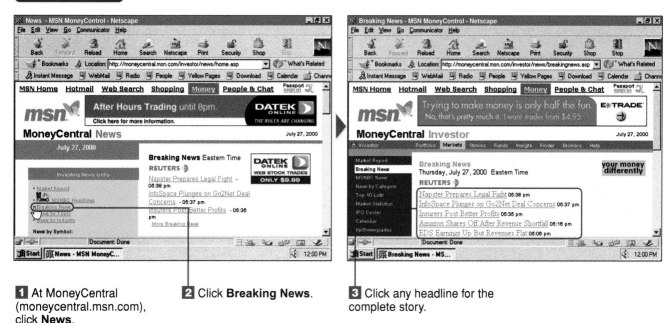

1 At MoneyCentral (moneycentral.msn.com), click **News**.

2 Click **Breaking News**.

3 Click any headline for the complete story.

SEARCH FOR STOCKS THAT MEET YOUR ETHICAL STANDARDS

Many people do not want their money going to companies that market products they do not approve of. Ethical Investing's Web site is an example of a site that can help you screen out investments according to political and moral standards.

SEARCH FOR STOCKS THAT MEET YOUR ETHICAL STANDARDS

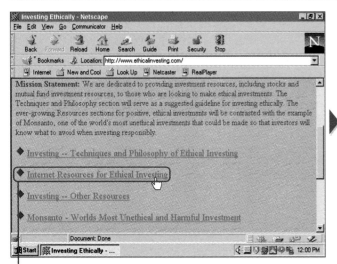

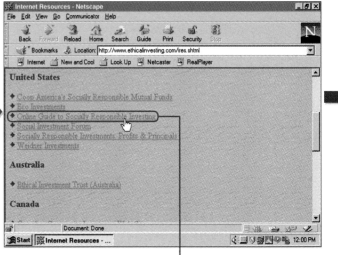

1 At Ethical Investing's Web site (www.ethicalinvesting.com), click **Internet Resources for Ethical Investing**.

Note: If you're interested in ethical investing in Australia, Canada, Germany, the Netherlands, or the United Kingdom, scroll down for more information.

2 Click **Online Guide to Socially Responsible Investing**.

? What sorts of ethical issues can I check about a company?

You can look for the issues you're most interested in. Most often, investors try to avoid companies that handle— depending on their political views— weapons, cigarettes, birth control products, or obscene books and movies. On the positive side, some ethical-issues screening sites look for companies with good environmental or labor records.

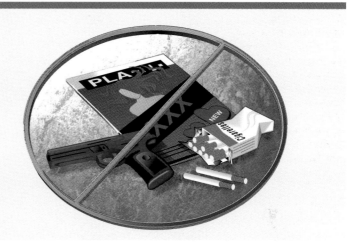

3 Click **SIF Directory**.

4 Scroll to the state you want to find out about, or leave the State entry on **Any** to cover all states.

5 Click the arrow below Category and scroll down to **Social Investment Research & Shareholder Activism**.

6 Click **Go**.

■ You get a list of organizations, their criteria, and links to their contact information and Web sites. Contact an organization you're interested in to see what investments it recommends.

DISCOVER WHICH NEW COMPANIES ARE HITTING THE MARKET

An *initial public offering* (IPO) marks the first time a company offers shares to the public. These offerings are too new to be included in the databases where you usually get stock prices. But you can find out about them from sites like IPO Monitor and IPO Data Systems.

PICK UP NEWS AND FILINGS FROM IPO MONITOR

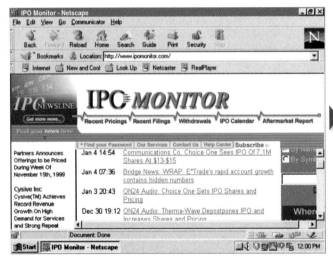

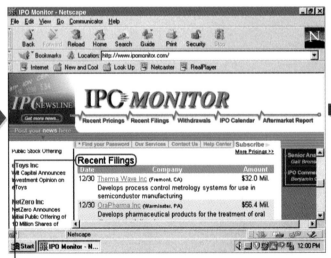

■ For starters, IPO Monitor (www.ipomonitor.com) offers headline news about newly public or about to be public companies.

1 Scroll down for more headlines.

2 Scroll down to **Recent Filings**.

■ **Recent Filings** lists companies that recently announced plans to go public.

3 Scroll down to **Hot IPOs**.

How risky are IPOs?

IPOs have no trading history, and the products, management, and company itself may be new and untested. In addition, IPOs tend to shoot up like a firecracker—and then crash just as dramatically. All that makes investing in IPOs a little like going fishing with a blindfold.

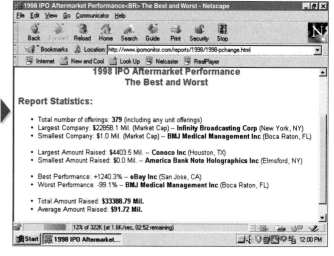

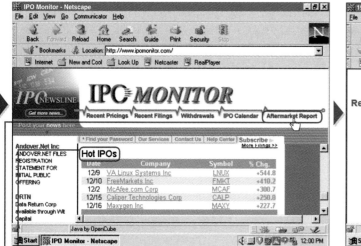

■ **Hot IPOs** lists recent IPOs whose prices have soared.

4 Click **Aftermarket Report**.

5 Select a report you're interested in (choose a coverage period and industry) on the next page. Then click **Go**.

Note: To view the reports, you need to subscribe to IPO Monitor.

■ A follow-up to see how IPOs have traded months after the original sale.

CONTINUED

It is very hard for an ordinary investor to get a crack at an IPO, because so many shares are reserved for corporate insiders and big institutional investors. So if you really want one of these, your best bet may be to use a full-service online broker that underwrites IPOs itself. Or you can jump in on *secondary trading*, buying—usually at a higher price—from people who bought shares at the initial public sale.

RESEARCH SPECIFIC IPOS ON IPO DATA SYSTEMS

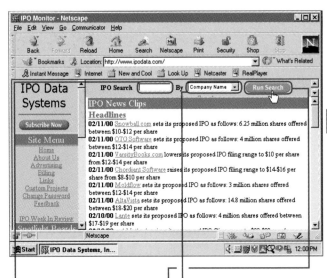

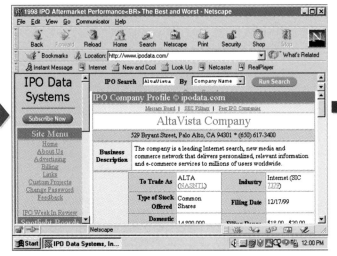

1 At IPO Data Systems (www.ipodata.com), type the company name or ticker symbol of the IPO you're interested in in the **IPO Search** box.

2 Hit the arrow at **By** and scroll to the way you want to search – by company name, by ticker symbol, and so on.

3 Click **Run Search**.

Note: To access some information, you need to subscribe to the Web site. You can access the IPO information under Headlines on the home page without a subscription.

■ The profile of an upcoming IPO

4 Scroll down for more information about the company.

What kind of information should I find out about an IPO?

An IPO is a stock. Therefore, you need the same kind of information as for any other stock.

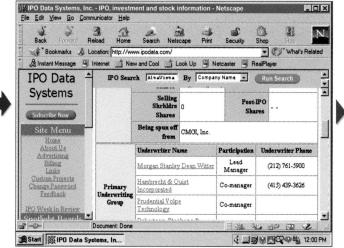

■ The offering's underwriters.

5 Scroll down for more information.

■ The income statement

6 Scroll down to see the balance sheet.

SET UP AN ONLINE ACCOUNT

Opening an online brokerage account is something like opening a bank account or applying for a credit card. This section uses the setup process at TD Waterhouse as an example.

1 At TD Waterhouse's home page (www.waterhouse.com), click **Open a New Account**.

2 Click the type of account you want.

3 Fill in the requested information about your name, address, and so on.

4 Click **Complete Online**.

5 On the next screen that appears, click **Yes** to confirm the information you inputted.

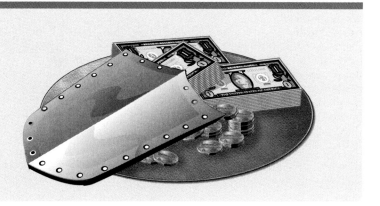

Why does the brokerage need all this information?

By law, a brokerage is required to "know its customers" so that it can steer them away from unsuitable investments. For instance, an elderly widow living on a small pension should probably not be putting a big portion of her savings into high-risk Internet startups.

6 Fill in the required information about your employment, Social Security number, how you prefer to be contacted, and so on.

7 Click **Next**.

8 Fill in the requested information about your bank account, accounts at other brokerages, whether you are employed by an exchange or brokerage, and whether you are a major shareholder.

9 Click **Next**.

CONTINUED

Completing an online application does not take much time. Before you can start trading, however, the brokerage has to review your information.

SET UP AN ONLINE ACCOUNT (CONTINUED)

10 Choose various account options, such as whether you want to trade with cash or on margin and whether you want dividends reinvested.

11 Click **Next**.

■ On the next two screens that appear, you may choose various types of money market funds.

12 Click **Yes** to trade online (O changes to ●).

13 Click **Next**.

How much money will I be required to keep in my account?

It can vary from $5,000 to zero. But if you maintain a high balance—at least $100,000—you may get special privileges.

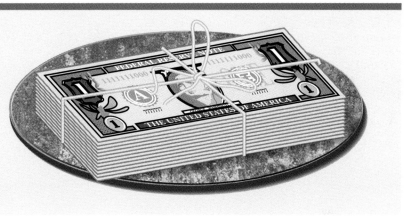

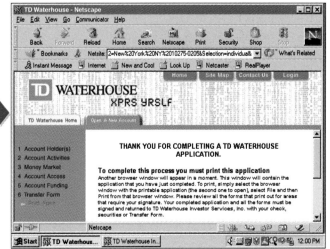

14 Click next to the way you want to submit your $1,000 minimum deposit.

15 Click **Next**.

■ On the next screen that appears, you can answer questions regarding whether anyone referred you to this site.

■ Print out and mail in the application, with your $1,000 deposit.

Note: At brokerages with no minimum deposit, you may be able to submit the application online.

BUY A STOCK ONLINE

After you finally sit down to buy or sell a stock online, it is incredibly easy. Here is how you would do a basic trade at DLJdirect.

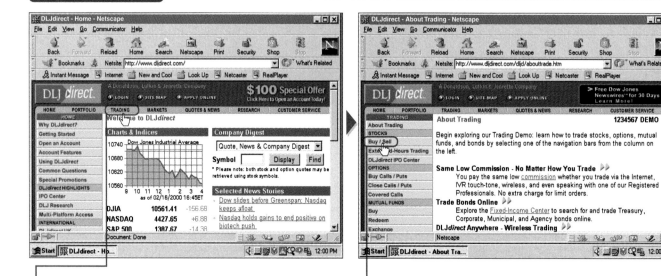

1 At DLJdirect (www.dljdirect.com), click **Trading**.

2 Click **Buy/Sell** under Stocks.

❓ What if I change my mind?

As long as the order has not yet been executed, you can probably cancel it. That means you have a decent chance of canceling a limit order, an excellent chance of canceling any order placed outside of normal trading hours, and no chance at all of canceling a market order placed during trading hours.

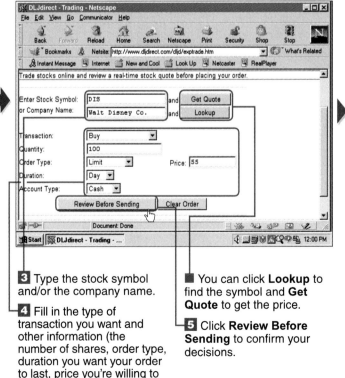

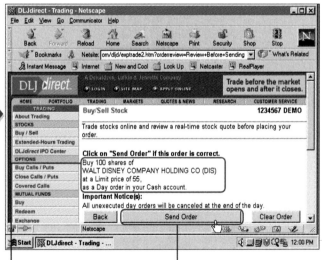

3 Type the stock symbol and/or the company name.

■ You can click **Lookup** to find the symbol and **Get Quote** to get the price.

4 Fill in the type of transaction you want and other information (the number of shares, order type, duration you want your order to last, price you're willing to trade at, and account type).

5 Click **Review Before Sending** to confirm your decisions.

■ A summary of your order

6 Click **Send Order** if everything is the way you want it.

CHAPTER 5

Trading Bonds Online

What kinds of bonds are on the market? What should you look for— yield, maturity, price? This chapter helps you sort through all the types of bonds available and explains how to buy bonds online.

UNDERSTAND HOW BONDS WORK

You can think of a *bond* as an IOU. When you buy a bond, you are actually lending money to the company or government that issued the bond.

TWO WAYS TO BUY A BOND

You can purchase bonds in two basic ways: as individual bonds from dealers—typically $5,000 worth at a time—or as an assortment of bonds in a mutual fund or unit investment trust.

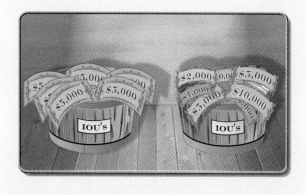

PRINCIPAL AND INTEREST

The company or government agency that issues the bonds promises to pay you back the principal at a fixed date. You will typically be paid interest at regular intervals until then. Because most of these payments are established—or fixed—in advance, bonds are also called *fixed-income securities*.

The two most common ways to pay interest are

- **Fixed rates:** These stay the same for the life of the bond.

- **Adjustable rates:** These rise or fall in accordance with prevailing market rates.

PUTS AND CALLS

Some bonds have *call* provisions that enable the issuer to repay the principal early or *put* provisions that allow investors to demand repayment early. Why would you want to get out early? If interest rates are rising or falling more than expected, the value of the interest payment on the bond will probably change accordingly.

MATURITY

The *maturity date* is the fixed date that the issuer of the bonds promises to pay you back the principal you lent it. As a general rule, short-term corporate bonds—actually, they are called *notes*—mature in four years or less. Medium-term bonds and notes go for 5 to 12 years. Long-term bonds have maturities of 12 years and longer.

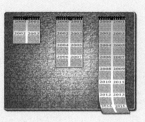

YIELD

The *interest rate* tells you only the rate at which you will be paid. *Yield* tells you how much you will actually take in. Yield is calculated by dividing the interest payments by the purchase price.

Say you buy a bond for $80 that pays interest at 6 percent. The annual yield on that bond is 6 divided by 80, or 7.5 percent of your purchase price.

The principle of risk and return is discussed in Chapter 2. Well, this principle also applies to bonds: Investors who buy bonds with a longer maturity keep their money at risk longer. Therefore, the interest rate and yield on long-term bonds are usually higher than for other types.

PRICE

Pricing is one of the great mysteries of the bond market. Each dealer sets its own price (adding in a markup for profit). Prices aren't posted in any central exchange, as stock quotes are.

INFLATION

Bonds do not like inflation and rising interest rates, because those conditions make their old, fixed rates less valuable.

DISTINGUISH BETWEEN THE TYPES OF BONDS AND OTHER FIXED-INCOME SECURITIES

Each bond issue has a unique structure in terms of maturity, yield, and other provisions. But bonds and other fixed-income securities can be classified by general types.

Bonds & Fixed-Income Securities

IOU U.S. Treasury Bills	IOU Municipal Bonds
IOU Money Market Funds	IOU Corporate Bonds
IOU Junk Bonds	IOU Asset-Backed Securities

U.S. TREASURY BILLS

How would you like Uncle Sam to owe you money for a change? The U.S. government borrows trillions of dollars through notes and bonds, usually at maturities ranging from three months to 30 years.

Most countries similarly borrow large amounts of money. Governments and other bond issuers use the rates on U.S. Treasury bonds as a benchmark for setting their own rates.

MUNICIPAL BONDS

The big advantage of *municipal bonds*—bonds and notes issued by U.S. states, cities, counties, and local government agencies and often called *munis*—is that they are usually exempt from income tax. They are also usually very creditworthy. In the entire history of the United States, only a few issuers have ever defaulted on municipal bonds.

MONEY MARKET FUNDS

Money market funds are a basket of ultra-safe, short-term, low interest-paying debt from issuers with top credit ratings. These funds can include U.S. government notes and bonds, municipal bonds, bank certificates of deposit, and corporate commercial paper.

CORPORATE BONDS

Borrowings by private companies are called *corporate bonds.* The bonds issued by large, well-known companies like General Motors or IBM—known as *blue chips*—are considered almost as solid as U.S. government paper. But companies that are less well known or that have financial problems pay higher interest rates to attract buyers.

JUNK BONDS

Junk bonds—or, as their issuers prefer to call them, *high-yield bonds*—are bonds with credit ratings below investment grade. The risk and yields are both high.

Why the disparaging name? Because sometimes these borrowers fall into such financial trouble that their IOUs indeed become as worthless as junk.

ASSET-BACKED SECURITIES

Take a collection of individual debts such as mortgages, put them together in a package, let investors buy a share of that package—and you have an *asset-backed security.* The investors get regular interest payments.

FIND OUT TREASURY BILL PRICES

The growth of trading on the Internet has forced the bond industry to start putting some of its secret pricing data online. A good source for information on U.S. government issues is www.Govpx.com, a database founded in 1990 by all the primary dealers of federal securities.

FIND OUT TREASURY BILL PRICES

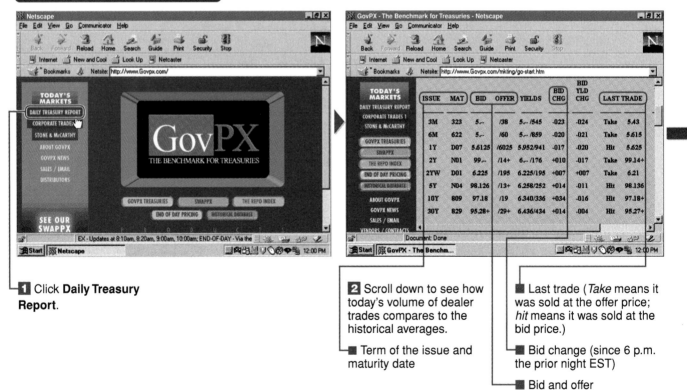

1 Click **Daily Treasury Report**.

2 Scroll down to see how today's volume of dealer trades compares to the historical averages.

■ Term of the issue and maturity date

■ Last trade (*Take* means it was sold at the offer price; *hit* means it was sold at the bid price.)

■ Bid change (since 6 p.m. the prior night EST)

■ Bid and offer

Which issues are considered short-term?

Those that mature in one year or less.

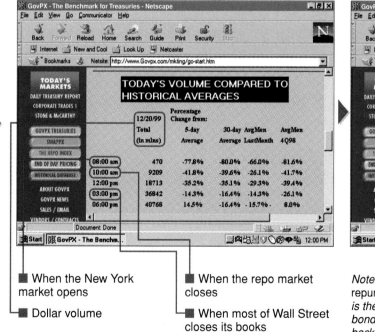

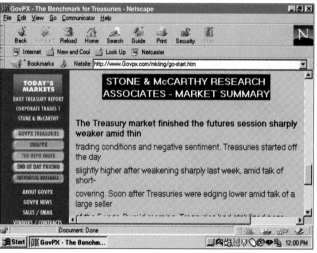

■ When the New York market opens

■ Dollar volume

■ When the repo market closes

■ When most of Wall Street closes its books

Note: Repo *stands for* repurchase agreement, *which is the temporary sale of a bond; the seller agrees to buy back the bond from the buyer at a stated price and time.*

3 Scroll down to see a summary of highlights of that day's bond market.

FIND OUT THE LATEST PRICES OF MUNICIPAL BONDS

Something like 1.5 million different issues of municipal bonds are currently outstanding. Bonds Online (www.bondsonline.com)—one of a number of databases for this market—draws its list from several hundred trading desks.

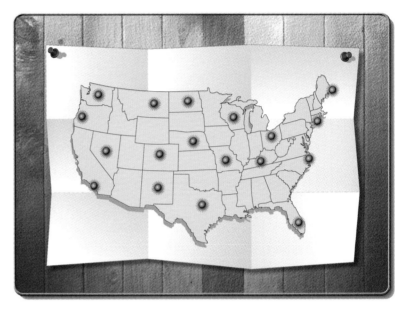

FIND OUT THE LATEST PRICES OF MUNICIPAL BONDS

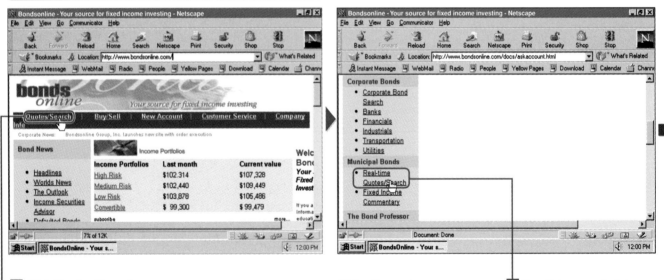

1 Click **Quotes/Search**.

■ On the next page, you may be asked if you have an account with the site. If you don't, you can still access the site's information.

2 Scroll down and click **Real-Time Quotes/Search** under Municipal Bonds.

What is the difference between a *G.O. bond* and a *revenue bond*?

A G.O. bond—short for *general obligation*—is backed by the full faith and credit of the government that issues it. A revenue bond is supported only by income from a specific source—for example, a toll road—so it is slightly less secure.

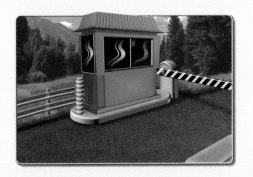

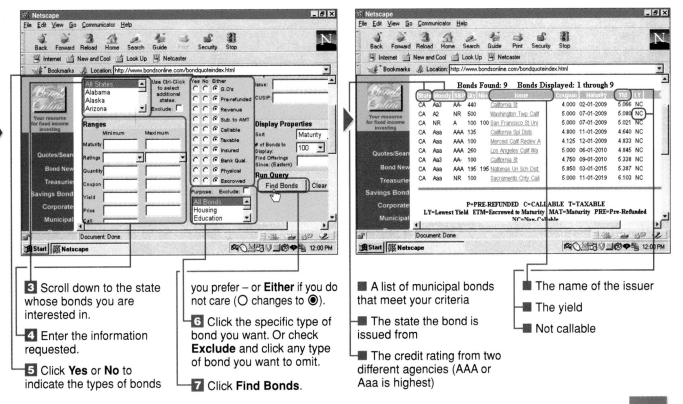

3 Scroll down to the state whose bonds you are interested in.

4 Enter the information requested.

5 Click **Yes** or **No** to indicate the types of bonds

you prefer – or **Either** if you do not care (O changes to ◉).

6 Click the specific type of bond you want. Or check **Exclude** and click any type of bond you want to omit.

7 Click **Find Bonds**.

■ A list of municipal bonds that meet your criteria

■ The state the bond is issued from

■ The credit rating from two different agencies (AAA or Aaa is highest)

■ The name of the issuer

■ The yield

■ Not callable

SEE WHAT'S AVAILABLE IN THE CORPORATE MARKET

The corporate market is far smaller than its municipal cousin, with just about 200,000 issues. But that is still nearly 30 times larger than the U.S. stock market.

SEE WHAT'S AVAILABLE IN THE CORPORATE MARKET

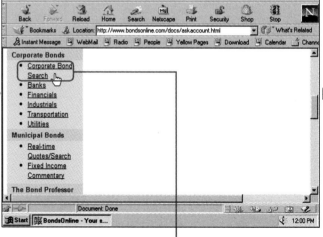

1 At Bonds Online (www.bondsonline.com), click **Quotes/Search**.

■ On the next page, you may be asked if you have an account with the site. If you don't, you can still access the site's information.

2 Scroll down and click **Corporate Bond Search** under Corporate Bonds.

? What features of a bond should I look at most closely?

Probably the two most important are *yield to maturity*, which tells you the total return you get if you hold the paper until it matures, and *credit rating*, which tells you how trustworthy the issuer is. You may also want to learn more about the company issuing the bonds by doing some of the research discussed in Chapter 4.

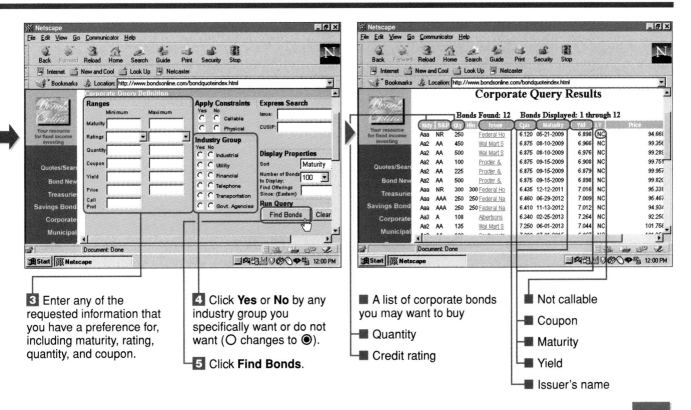

3 Enter any of the requested information that you have a preference for, including maturity, rating, quantity, and coupon.

4 Click **Yes** or **No** by any industry group you specifically want or do not want (O changes to ●).

5 Click **Find Bonds**.

■ A list of corporate bonds you may want to buy

■ Quantity

■ Credit rating

■ Not callable

■ Coupon

■ Maturity

■ Yield

■ Issuer's name

BUY BONDS ONLINE

Because of the vast number of different bonds and the lack of a central exchange, online bond trading started far later than stock trading. This example uses the trading program at DLJdirect (www.dljdirect.com) to show how to buy bonds online, but you can buy and sell bonds through almost any big online brokerage.

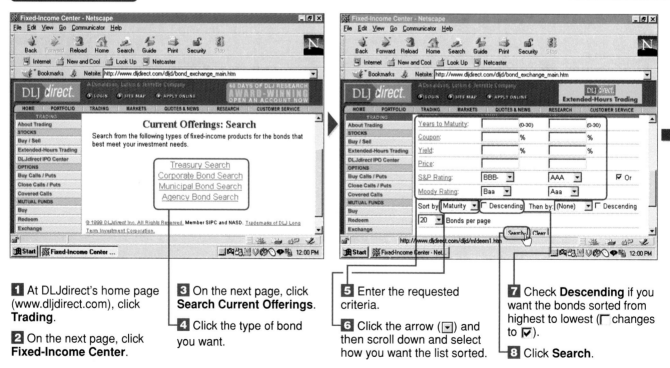

1 At DLJdirect's home page (www.dljdirect.com), click **Trading**.

2 On the next page, click **Fixed-Income Center**.

3 On the next page, click **Search Current Offerings**.

4 Click the type of bond you want.

5 Enter the requested criteria.

6 Click the arrow (▾) and then scroll down and select how you want the list sorted.

7 Check **Descending** if you want the bonds sorted from highest to lowest (☐ changes to ☑).

8 Click **Search**.

Should I buy corporate or municipal bonds?

Generally, municipal bonds pay slightly lower yields than corporate bonds of the same quality because their tax-exemption saves you money on taxes. The higher your tax bracket, the more you probably need a tax shelter like muni bonds.

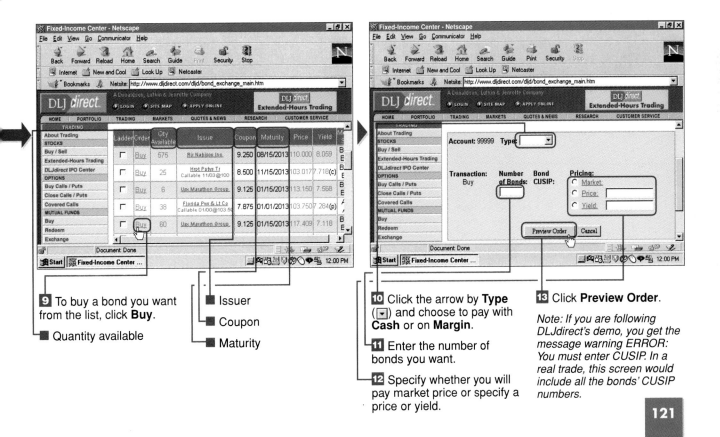

9 To buy a bond you want from the list, click **Buy**.

■ Quantity available

■ Issuer

■ Coupon

■ Maturity

10 Click the arrow by **Type** ([▼]) and choose to pay with **Cash** or on **Margin**.

11 Enter the number of bonds you want.

12 Specify whether you will pay market price or specify a price or yield.

13 Click **Preview Order**.

Note: If you are following DLJdirect's demo, you get the message warning ERROR: You must enter CUSIP. In a real trade, this screen would include all the bonds' CUSIP numbers.

CHAPTER 6

Trading Mutual Funds Online

What sorts of mutual funds are there? What fees do they charge? This chapter shows you the online world of mutual funds.

UNDERSTAND HOW MUTUAL FUNDS WORK

Experts say you should diversify your investments, but you probably don't have enough money to buy a whole lot of different stocks and bonds. The solution for you may be to invest in mutual funds.

WHAT IS A MUTUAL FUND?

You can think of a *mutual fund* as a basket of investments. The fund takes in money from thousands of shareholders and uses that money to invest in a diversified portfolio. Each fund has a specialty—for instance, small-cap stocks or emerging growth stocks or municipal bonds—and may hold dozens of securities of that specialty.

WHAT DO YOU REALLY OWN?

When you buy a share of a mutual fund, you do not buy any particular stock or bond. You buy a piece of the basket.

LOADS AND FEES

Mutual funds charge two basic kinds of fees:

- **Shareholder fees, or *loads:*** These are special charges for buying or selling your mutual fund shares. A *front-end load* is for buying, and a *back-end load,* or deferred sales charge, is for selling. Front-end loads typically range from 3 percent of the initial investment to the legal maximum of 8.5 percent. Back-end loads vary, but they're generally a percentage of the fund's net asset value (or price per share), reaching as high as 6 percent and declining gradually to zero if you hold the fund for several years.

  Only some funds have these charges. So, all things being equal, you should probably look for *no-load* funds.

- **Operating expense fees:** These are fees that all funds charge every year, and they are supposed to cover the cost of running the portfolio. They include the management fee, paid to the manager who makes the investment decisions, and the 12b-1 fee, to pay for marketing. These fees are always a percentage of the total net value of the fund's assets—perhaps 0.2 percent to 2 percent.

CLASSES AND SHARES

Funds may be broken down into different classes—Class A, Class B, all the way to Class Z. These simply represent various ways of paying for shares: Class A usually represents front-end loads, Class B back-end loads, and so on.

DISTINGUISH BETWEEN DIFFERENT TYPES OF MUTUAL FUNDS

You can find a mutual fund for just about every type of stock or bond you can think of, plus several specialty types.

INCOME FUNDS VERSUS GROWTH FUNDS

Income funds look for established companies that can be relied on for stable prices and steady dividends.

Growth funds take more risk, buying stocks on the anticipation of rising prices.

BALANCED FUNDS

Balanced funds give you even more diversification by investing in a mix of stocks and bonds. They try to juggle three goals: income, growth, and preservation of capital.

INDEX FUNDS

Index funds buy stocks that resemble the holdings of any of the major indexes that are used to measure the markets, such as the Standard & Poor's 500 stock index. The theory is that you cannot beat the market, so you may as well just try to copy it.

They also tend to charge lower fees than actively managed funds.

SPECIALIZED INDEX FUNDS

Specialized index funds follow the principle of index funds, buying stocks that mirror a particular index. But they also use some discretionary judgment by picking out particular specialized markets to mirror—often ones that are underrepresented in the big indexes.

CONCENTRATED FUNDS

"Keep it small" is the philosophy of *concentrated* funds. If you have found a few terrific stocks, why throw money into a lot of other holdings that will not do as well just for the sake of diversification?

Typically, a concentrated fund holds 20 or fewer stocks sharing certain characteristics; for example, the fund may buy only midsize undervalued stocks.

SECTOR FUNDS

Sector funds represent another way of specializing— by investing in only a single industry. Health care and technology are the two most popular sectors.

AFFINITY FUNDS

Affinity funds and *socially responsible* funds try to appeal to buyers' hobbies or political views. For example, there have been funds that buy only sports-related investments or only stocks approved by a board of Catholic activists.

Chapter 4 discusses socially responsible investing in more detail.

SEE WHAT KINDS OF FUNDS ARE AVAILABLE

Go to any mutual fund company's Web site and see what products it lists to get a sense of just how many funds are out there. This chapter uses Vanguard Group as an example because it is one of the two largest fund families in the United States (Fidelity Investments being the other).

SEE WHAT KINDS OF FUNDS ARE AVAILABLE

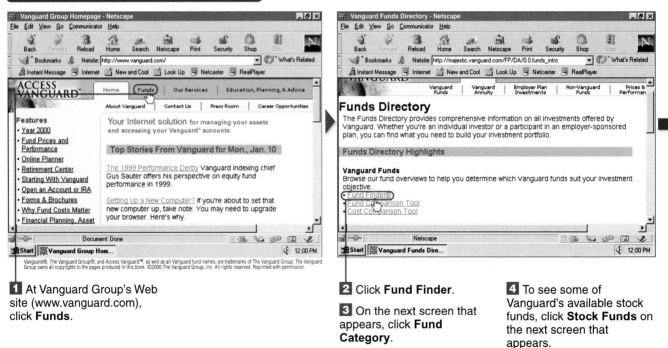

1 At Vanguard Group's Web site (www.vanguard.com), click **Funds**.

2 Click **Fund Finder**.

3 On the next screen that appears, click **Fund Category**.

4 To see some of Vanguard's available stock funds, click **Stock Funds** on the next screen that appears.

How many different categories of funds are there?

The Investment Company Institute (the major trade group for the mutual fund industry) divides funds into 33 different categories, according to their investment objectives.

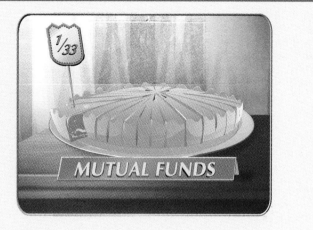

Vanguard Fund Finder Fund Category, Symbol View - Netscape

Stock Funds—General Stock		
Fund	Fund Symbol	Fund Number
Vanguard Convertible Securities Fund	VCVSX	0082
Vanguard Equity Income Fund	VEIPX	0065
Vanguard Growth and Income Fund	VQNPX	0093
Vanguard Growth Index Fund	VIGRX	0009
Vanguard Growth Index Fund Institutional Shares	VIGIX	0868
Vanguard Institutional Index Fund	VINIX	0094
Vanguard Institutional Index Fund Plus Shares	VIIIX	0854
Vanguard Morgan Growth Fund	VMRGX	0026
Vanguard Tax-Managed Capital Appreciation Fund	VMCAX	0102
Vanguard Tax-Managed Capital Appreciation Fund Institutional Shares	VTCIX	0135
Vanguard Tax-Managed Growth and Income Fund	VTGIX	0101

Document: Done

Start | Vanguard Fund Finde... | 12:00 PM

Vanguard Fund Finder Fund Category, Symbol View - Netscape

Vanguard 500 Index Fund	VFINX	0040
Stock Funds—More Aggressive		
Fund	Fund Symbol	Fund Number
Vanguard Aggressive Growth Fund	VHAGX	0114
Vanguard Capital Opportunity Fund	VHCOX	0111
Vanguard Explorer Fund	VEXPX	0024
Vanguard Extended Market Index Fund	VEXMX	0098
Vanguard Extended Market Index Fund Institutional Shares	VIEIX	0856
Vanguard Mid-Cap Index Fund	VIMSX	0859
Vanguard Mid-Cap Index Fund Institutional Shares	VMCIX	0864
Vanguard PRIMECAP Fund	VPMCX	0059
Vanguard Selected Value Fund	VASVX	0934
Vanguard Small-Cap Growth Index Fund	VISGX	0861
Vanguard Small-Cap Growth Index Fund Institutional Shares	---	0866

http://majestic2.vanguard.com/FP/DA/0.1.vgi_FProfileSnaps

Start | Vanguard Fund Finde... | 12:00 PM

■ A partial list of Vanguard's U.S. general stock funds. You can click any fund name to get more information on that fund.

5 Scroll down to see different types of stock funds.

■ Some of Vanguard's more aggressive U.S. stock funds

6 Scroll down to see more types of stock funds.

CONTINUED

SEE WHAT KINDS OF FUNDS ARE AVAILABLE

(CONTINUED)

There are thousands of different mutual funds. And more are started—and shut down—every year.

SEE WHAT KINDS OF FUNDS ARE AVAILABLE (CONTINUED)

Vanguard Fund Finder Fund Category, Symbol View - Netscape

File Edit View Go Communicator Help

Back | Forward | Reload | Home | Search | Netscape | Print | Security | Shop | Stop

Bookmarks | Netsite: nds&SortFundsBy=Type&FundsReportView=Symbol&VgiFund=1 | What's Related

Instant Message | Internet | New and Cool | Look Up | Netcaster | RealPlayer

Vanguard U.S. Growth Fund | VWUSX | 0023

Stock Funds—Industry Specific

Fund	Fund Symbol	Fund Number
Vanguard Energy Fund	VGENX	0051
Vanguard Gold and Precious Metals Fund	VGPMX	0053
Vanguard Health Care Fund	VGHCX	0052
Vanguard REIT Index Fund	VGSIX	0123
Vanguard Utilities Income Fund	VGSUX	0057

Stock Funds—International/Global

Fund	Fund Symbol	Fund Number
Vanguard Emerging Markets Stock Index Fund	VEIEX	0533
Vanguard European Stock Index Fund	VEURX	0079
Vanguard Global Equity Fund	VHGEX	0129
Vanguard International Growth Fund	VWIGX	0081

Netscape

Start | Vanguard Fund Finde... | 12:00 PM

Vanguard Fund Finder Fund Category, Symbol View - Netscape

File Edit View Go Communicator Help

Back | Forward | Reload | Home | Search | Netscape | Print | Security | Shop | Stop

Bookmarks | Netsite: nds&SortFundsBy=Type&FundsReportView=Symbol&VgiFund=1 | What's Related

Instant Message | Internet | New and Cool | Look Up | Netcaster | RealPlayer

Vanguard Total Bond Market Index Fund Institutional Shares | VBTIX | 0222

Bond Funds—Taxable Long-Term

Fund	Fund Symbol	Fund Number
Vanguard Admiral Long-Term Treasury Fund	VALGX	0020
Vanguard Long-Term Bond Index Fund	VBLTX	0522
Vanguard Long-Term Corporate Fund	VWESX	0028
Vanguard Long-Term Treasury Fund	VUSTX	0083
Vanguard Preferred Stock Fund	VQIIX	0038

Bond Funds—Tax-Exempt National

Fund	Fund Symbol	Fund Number
Vanguard High-Yield Tax-Exempt Fund	VWAHX	0044
Vanguard Insured Long-Term Tax-Exempt Fund	VILPX	0058
Vanguard Intermediate-Term Tax-Exempt Fund	VWITX	0042
Vanguard Limited-Term Tax-Exempt Fund	VMLTX	0031
Vanguard Long-Term Tax-Exempt Fund	VWLTX	0043

Document: Done

Start | Vanguard Fund Finde... | 12:00 PM

■ Some of Vanguard's sector and global funds

7 To see some of Vanguard's available bond funds, click **Bond Funds** at the top of the page.

■ Some of Vanguard's bond funds

8 To see some of Vanguard's available money market funds, click **Money Markets** at the top of the page.

How are balanced funds split between stocks and bonds?

The split varies from fund to fund. You can choose among balanced funds with different levels of risk—just the way you can choose among stock funds—with the riskier funds generally having more stock investments and the less risky funds having more bond investments.

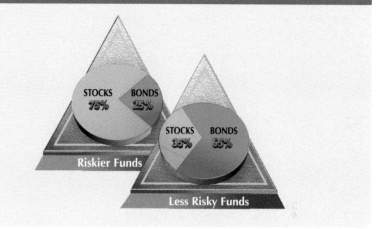

■ Some of Vanguard's money market funds

9 To see some of Vanguard's available balanced funds, click **Balanced Funds** at the top of the page.

■ Some of Vanguard's balanced funds

FIND OUT DETAILS ABOUT A FUND

For any mutual fund, you want to know its investment philosophy, its risk level, its fees, its returns, and what yardstick to measure its returns by.

FIND OUT DETAILS ABOUT A FUND

1 Follow the steps in the section "Seeing What Kinds of Funds Are Available" and select a fund you may be interested in.

*Note: To find out the details of Vanguard's Aggressive Growth Fund (shown here), click **Funds** at*

*Vanguard's Web site (www.vanguard.com), click **Fund Finder**, and then click **Vanguard Aggressive Growth Fund**.*

■ The fund's objective

■ The fund's risk level

■ The minimum amount you must start with

?

How can I tell if a fund's returns are any good?

To be fair, you should compare your fund with an index that is geared to the same types of investments and the same level of risk. The most widely used indexes are Standard & Poor's 500 (large-cap U.S. stocks), the Wilshire 5000 (pretty much the entire U.S. equity market), and the Russell 2000 (small-cap U.S. stocks).

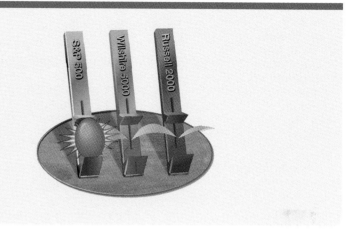

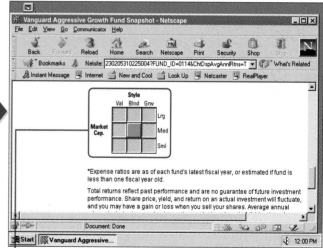

■ Returns so far this year

■ Returns over time, compared with an appropriate index

■ How this fund fits in a style box that categorizes the fund by market cap and broad investment style

After you settle on an investment style, you should compare the funds that follow that style. You can look up the data on independent services, such as Morningstar.com.

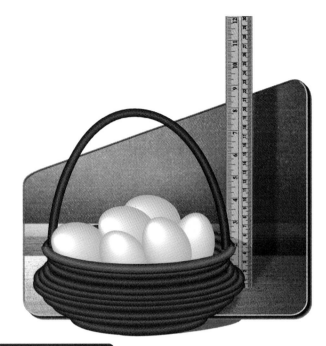

FIND OUT WHICH FUNDS HAVE PERFORMED BEST

1 At Morningstar.com (www.morningstar.com), scroll down to **Tool Box**, on the left.

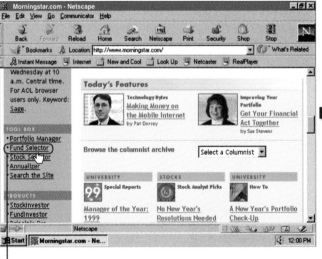

2 Click **Fund Selector**.

What time period should I look at?

Go back as far as you can—a year, at least.

3 Click the arrow (▼) by **Preset Criteria** and scroll down to choose a broad category (U.S. stocks, bonds, and so on). OR scroll down, specify your criteria, and click **Show Results**.

■ Morningstar.com returns a list of funds.

■ You can change to one of four different views: **Snapshot, Performance, Portfolio,** or **Nuts & Bolts**.

CONTINUED ▶

Because returns should increase with risk, you need to compare funds in terms of risk level, too.

FIND OUT WHICH FUNDS HAVE PERFORMED BEST (CONTINUED)

Fund Name	Morningstar Category	Category Rating	Morningstar Rating	YTD Return (%)	Expense Ratio (%)	Net Assets ($ mil)
Small Growth Average				25.69	1.67	368
1st Source Monogram Sp	Small Growth	❷	★★	20.63	1.27	27
AAL Small Cap Stock A	Small Growth	❷	★★	10.95	1.82	178
AAL Small Cap Stock B	Small Growth	❷	★★	10.73	2.89	24
ABN AMRO Small Cap Gro	Small Growth	❶	★	9.60	1.17	73
ABN AMRO Small Cap Gro	Small Growth	❶	★	9.46	1.63	1
AIM Aggressive Growth	Small Growth	❸	★★★★	35.67	1.06	4,522
AIM Aggressive Growth	Small Growth	--	--	35.41	0.86	121
AIM Aggressive Growth	Small Growth	--	--	35.43	1.14	35
AIM Capital Developmen	Small Growth	❸	★★★	26.54	1.28	832
AIM Capital Developmen	Small Growth	❶	★★★★	26.32	2.02	661

Fund Name	Morningstar Category	Category Rating	Morningstar Rating	YTD Return (%)	Expense Ratio (%)	Net Assets ($ mil)
Large Growth Average				2.82	1.46	1,236
ABN AMRO Growth Comm	Large Growth	❶	★★★	-3.15	1.06	193
ABN AMRO Growth Inv	Large Growth	❶	★★★	-3.29	1.52	4
AIM Global Consumer Pr	Large Growth	❸	★★★★★	2.01	1.93	89
AIM Global Consumer Pr	Large Growth	❸	★★★★	--	1.43	1
AIM Global Consumer Pr	Large Growth	❸	★★★★★	1.87	2.43	128
AIM Global Consumer Pr	Large Growth	--	--	4.29	1.53	1
AIM Global Trends A	Large Growth	--	--	2.98	0.50	22
AIM Global Trends Adv	Large Growth	--	--	--	0.00	1
AIM Global Trends B	Large Growth	--	--	2.88	1.00	30
AIM Global Trends C	Large Growth	--	--	2.88	1.00	1

■ A list of small-cap growth funds

■ Check the Morningstar rating for the fund's risk level.

■ A list of large-cap growth funds

4 To search for just a specific rating, click your browser's **Back** button to return to the Set Criteria page.

? How can I include risk in my analysis?

Morningstar uses returns and risk to create its "star" system. Funds get five stars—the highest ranking—if they score in the top 10 percent of their investment category. Funds in the next 22.5 percent get four stars; the middle 35 percent, three stars; the next 22.5 percent, two stars; and the bottom 10 percent, just one star.

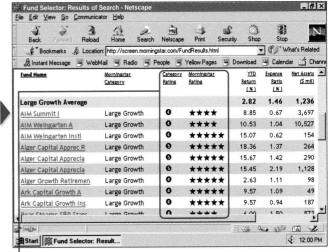

5 In the **Ratings and Risk** section, check the Morningstar Category and Star ratings you want to search for.

6 Select the risk level you want to search for (such as Low, Below Average, and so on).

7 Click **Show Results**.

■ Morningstar.com returns a list of funds with only the ratings you specified.

BUY MUTUAL FUND SHARES ONLINE

Although you probably will not trade your mutual funds as often as you trade stocks, you may occasionally want to buy or redeem shares or shift your allocations among various funds. To a limited degree, you can do these transactions online.

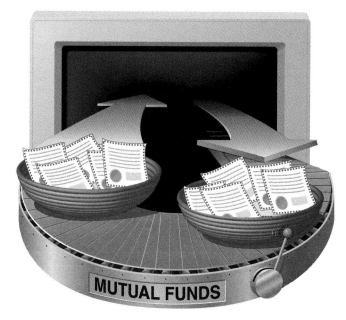

BUY MUTUAL FUND SHARES ONLINE

1 At Vanguard Group's Web site (www.vanguard.com), click **Your Accounts**.

2 Click **Log On**.

Can I get a prospectus online?

Depending on the fund and your computer's capabilities, you may not be able to access the *prospectus*—a long, dense document that explains the fund's investment objectives, fees, strategy, and riskiness. For that matter, you may prefer to read something this daunting on paper. However you do it, you should at least leaf through the prospectus. Most sites have a link where you can electronically download the prospectus or request a copy by mail.

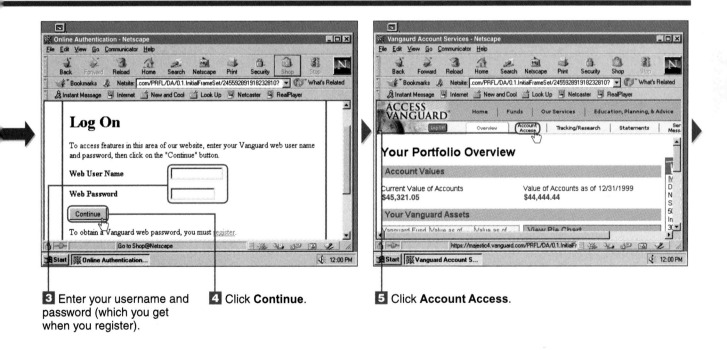

3 Enter your username and password (which you get when you register).

4 Click **Continue**.

5 Click **Account Access**.

CONTINUED

To buy mutual fund shares online, you need a way to get your money to the mutual fund company. At Vanguard Group, you can establish a special electronic account or an auto-draft arrangement with your bank. Or, of course, you can mail in a check.

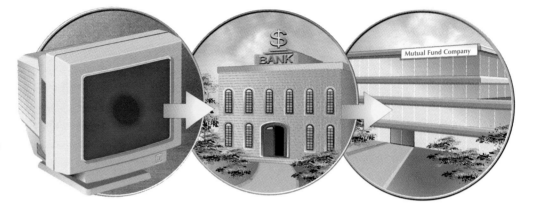

BUY MUTUAL FUND SHARES ONLINE (CONTINUED)

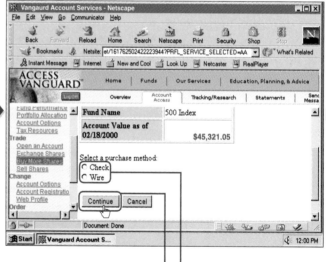

6 On the left side of the next screen, click **Buy More Shares**.

■ An explanation of the various ways to send money to Vanguard appears.

7 Click **Continue**.

8 On the next page, click on the number of the account to which you want to add shares.

9 On the next page, which warns you about possible fees, click **Continue**.

10 Check the circle next to your preferred purchase method: **Check** or **Wire** (○ changes to ●).

11 Click **Continue**.

What if I want to buy shares in several accounts?

You just have to perform the purchases one at a time.

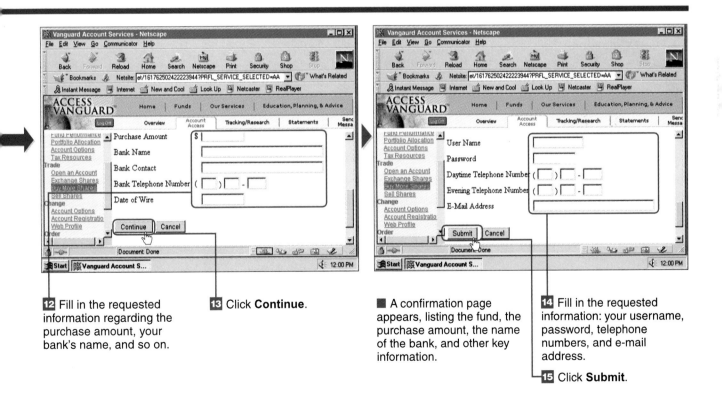

12 Fill in the requested information regarding the purchase amount, your bank's name, and so on.

13 Click **Continue**.

■ A confirmation page appears, listing the fund, the purchase amount, the name of the bank, and other key information.

14 Fill in the requested information: your username, password, telephone numbers, and e-mail address.

15 Click **Submit**.

TRANSFER MONEY BETWEEN MUTUAL FUNDS

Transferring assets from one fund to another is one of the easiest things to do online.

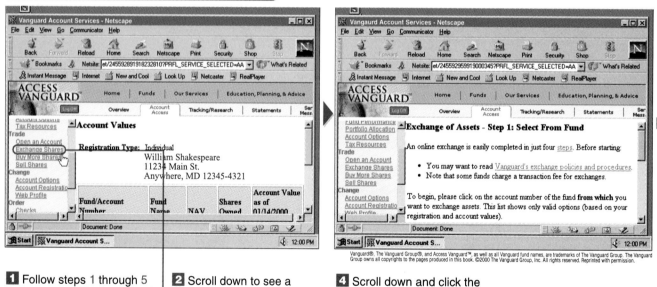

1 Follow steps 1 through 5 in the section "Buying Mutual Fund Shares Online."

2 Scroll down to see a summary of your holdings.

3 Click **Exchange Shares**.

4 Scroll down and click the account from which you want to take money out.

Will I have to pay a fee for transferring assets?

That depends on the fund. Often, funds charge fees only for shares held less than one year or less than five years, in order to encourage long-term investing.

5 Scroll down and click **Continue.**

6 Enter the amount you want to take out.

7 Click the circle by **Dollars, Shares,** or **Percent** (○ changes to ◉).

8 Click **Continue.**

9 On the screen that pops up with a list of your other Vanguard accounts, click the one you want to transfer the money to.

CHAPTER 7

Buying Real Estate Online

What kind of details about a property can you find out on the Internet? Can you actually buy a house without seeing it in person? This chapter shows you how to go house-hunting and even apply for a mortgage online.

BUY REAL ESTATE AS AN INVESTMENT

A house or an apartment can be more than a shelter to live in. It can also be a way to earn some income.

RENTING VERSUS BUYING

When you rent a house or apartment, your rent money disappears every month. All it pays for is maintaining the roof over your head.

BUYING YOUR OWN HOME

When you own the home you live in, your mortgage payment does double duty. Your home becomes an investment, just like a stock or bond, and you should get your money back—with a little profit added—when you sell it.

Of course, as with any investment, you also take a risk that you may lose money if you sell in a down market.

BUYING A SECOND HOME

Do you like to vacation in the same place frequently? Then consider buying a vacation home there—especially if it is a popular spot. This can be a good investment in several ways:

- Over time, a vacation home may well prove cheaper than staying in a motel or rental house year after year.
- During all the weeks that you don't use the house, you could make money by renting it to other vacationers.
- Eventually, if you decide to sell the property, you may earn back more than you paid for it.

BUYING RENTAL PROPERTY

You can buy and then rent out property that you never live in. For example, you may purchase a two-family house, take one part for yourself, and have tenants in the other half.

JOINING A PARTNERSHIP

If you want a really big investment, you could join with other passive investors in an partnership that buys apartment buildings, offices, or warehouses. Typically, these partnerships hire professional managers to run the property day to day.

Another option is to buy real estate almost like a stock, by taking a stake in a real estate investment trust, or REIT, that owns and manages many properties.

SELECT A NEIGHBORHOOD

How would you go about looking for a house if you don't know anything about the area where you're looking? For example, say that you've just gotten a job transfer to Silicon Valley and you want to buy a house.

A number of Web sites, usually run by major real estate firms or industry groups, list hundreds of thousands of homes and neighborhoods of all types across the United States and sometimes Canada, which you can look up according to several different categories. This chapter uses one of the first and largest sites as an example—Realtor.com.

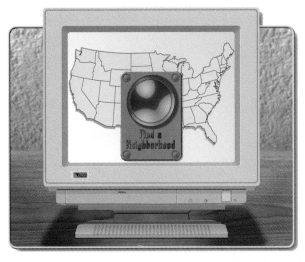

(If you have already pinpointed a neighborhood where you want to buy, you can skip ahead to the section "Find a House in the Neighborhood You Want.")

SELECT A NEIGHBORHOOD

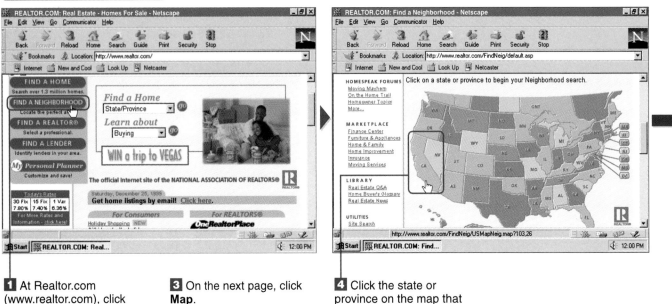

1 At Realtor.com (www.realtor.com), click **Find a Neighborhood**.

2 On the next page, click **I'm Not a Real Estate Professional/Find Me a Neighborhood**.

3 On the next page, click **Map**.

4 Click the state or province on the map that you are interested in (such as California).

How can the Internet help me buy a house?

It can save you time. By browsing through online listings, you can pinpoint some neighborhoods or even particular houses that you want to visit in person—and eliminate others.

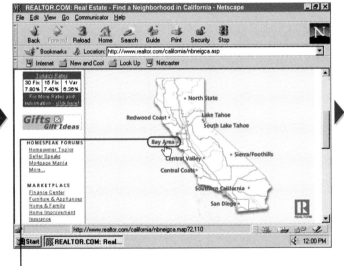

5 Click the general area you want on the map (such as the Bay Area).

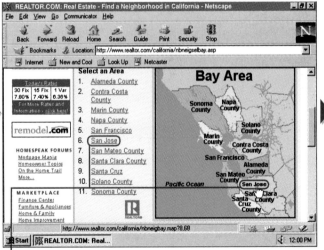

6 Click the city or local area you want on the map or from the list on the left (such as San Jose).

CONTINUED

When choosing a neighborhood, you probably have to compromise on some of your criteria in order to get what you want in other aspects. So you have to decide what is most important to you, whether it's the quality of the schools, the crime rate, the demographics, the price range, or the types of homes available.

SELECT A NEIGHBORHOOD (CONTINUED)

7 On the next page, click **Go Directly to Neighborhood Criteria**.

8 Click the arrow next to each neighborhood feature and then scroll down and choose the criteria you want or rate the importance of the feature on a scale of 1 to 5.

9 Scroll down for home features.

10 Click the arrow next to each home feature and then scroll down and specify the size, price, and such for that feature.

11 When you are finished, click **Find Neighborhoods in Map Area**.

?

How can I find a new neighborhood like the one I live in now?

On the Realtor.com site, you can input your current zip code in order to search for another zip code with similar characteristics. Of course, you may not get a very close match.

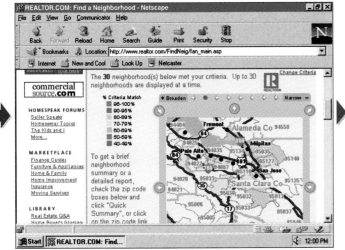

Note: The neighborhoods in red and orange most closely match your criteria. Check the Criteria Match chart to find how closely all the colors fit your needs.

12 Scroll down and click the zip code link of any neighborhood you are interested in to get more details.

■ How the neighborhood you chose stacks up against your criteria

FIND A HOUSE IN THE NEIGHBORHOOD YOU WANT

If you already know what
neighborhood you want to
buy in, you can start your
search for a house right
from Realtor.com's home
page (www.realtor.com).

Perhaps you want to buy a
cabin in Vermont to rent
out during ski season and
use for your own vacation
in summer.

FIND A HOUSE IN THE NEIGHBORHOOD YOU WANT

1 Click the arrow next to
State/Province and scroll to
the state or province you
want.

2 Click **Go**.

3 Click the arrow next to
Select an Area and scroll to
the area you want.

4 Click **Go**.

What qualities should I consider in a new neighborhood or new house?

You have to decide that for yourself. The Realtor.com Web site suggests some criteria you may consider, such as the quality of the local schools and whether there are a lot of children. Then there is the old saying that the three most important factors in real estate are "location, location, location."

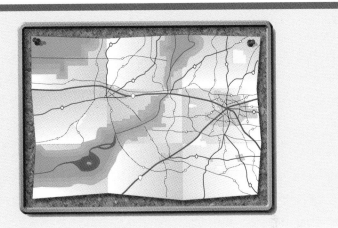

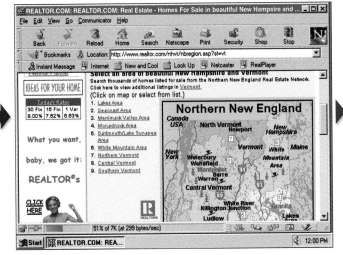

5 Click the area on the map you are interested in.

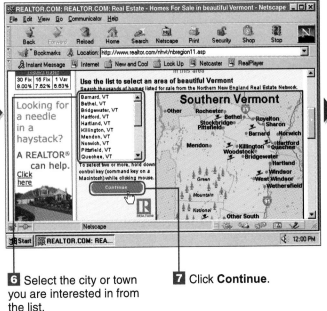

6 Select the city or town you are interested in from the list.

7 Click **Continue**.

CONTINUED

FIND A HOUSE IN THE NEIGHBORHOOD YOU WANT
(CONTINUED)

Searching real estate listings online can give you a good sense of the market. But there is no substitute for actually visiting the property itself.

FIND A HOUSE IN THE NEIGHBORHOOD YOU WANT (CONTINUED)

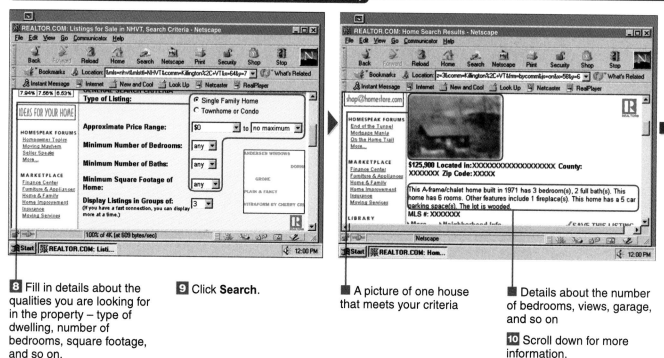

8 Fill in details about the qualities you are looking for in the property – type of dwelling, number of bedrooms, square footage, and so on.

9 Click **Search**.

■ A picture of one house that meets your criteria

■ Details about the number of bedrooms, views, garage, and so on

10 Scroll down for more information.

?

What if I do not like any of the listings that I get from one of these programs?

You can wait a week or so until more listings come on the market and try again. Or you can broaden your criteria—by raising your maximum price, for example.

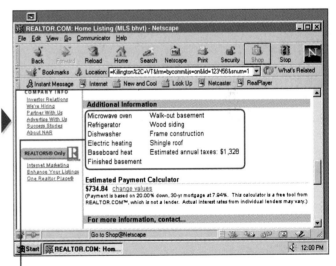

■ The **Estimated Payment Calculator** figures out your mortgage payments based on standard mortgage terms.

11 To contact the realtor listing the property, click the realtor's name or e-mail address.

12 For more information about the listing, click **More**.

■ Some features of the house (whether it has air conditioning, a fireplace, and so on)

DISCOVER WHAT MORTGAGES ARE AVAILABLE ONLINE

You can go to several Web sites to compare mortgage loan rates and, at some of them, actually apply for a mortgage right at your computer. This chapter shows you how to do both, using the E-Loan Web site as an example.

DISCOVER WHAT MORTGAGES ARE AVAILABLE ONLINE

1 At the E-Loan Web site (www.eloan.com), click **Home Purchase**.

2 Click next to the term of the mortgage you are seeking (☐ changes to ☑).

3 Enter the size of the loan you want.

4 Scroll down.

What are closing costs?

These are a smattering of extra charges relating to the purchase of a house, including mortgage insurance, title search and title insurance to prove the seller's ownership, taxes, and lawyers' fees. They can add up to thousands of dollars.

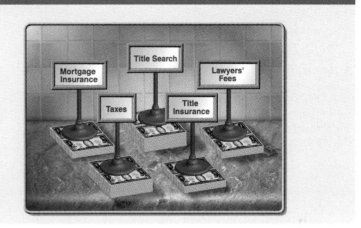

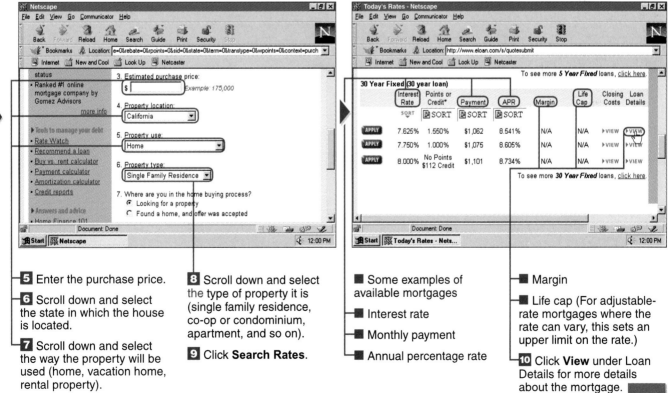

5 Enter the purchase price.

6 Scroll down and select the state in which the house is located.

7 Scroll down and select the way the property will be used (home, vacation home, rental property).

8 Scroll down and select the type of property it is (single family residence, co-op or condominium, apartment, and so on).

9 Click **Search Rates**.

■ Some examples of available mortgages

■ Interest rate

■ Monthly payment

■ Annual percentage rate

■ Margin

■ Life cap (For adjustable-rate mortgages where the rate can vary, this sets an upper limit on the rate.)

10 Click **View** under Loan Details for more details about the mortgage.

PREQUALIFY AND APPLY
FOR A MORTGAGE ONLINE

When you try to qualify
for a mortgage, lenders
want to look closely at
your income and your
other debts to determine
if you are creditworthy.
That means answering
the same questions
electronically that you
previously would have
answered on paper.

DETERMINE IF YOU QUALIFY FOR A MORTGAGE

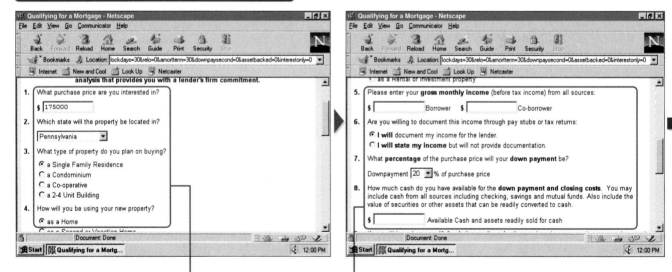

1 At the E-Loan Web site
(www.eloan.com), scroll
down to the bottom of the
page and click **Calculators
& Tools**.

2 Click **Get Pre-Qualified**.

3 Fill in all the requested
information about the type of
house you want to buy.

4 Scroll down.

5 Fill in the requested
information about your
income, the size of your
expected down payment, the
amount of ready cash you
have available, and so on.

6 Scroll down.

What if I'm turned down for a mortgage?

You can always try another bank or mortgage broker. Also, more money usually improves your chances: You could put in a larger down payment or pay a higher interest rate.

7 Fill in the requested information about your debts.

8 Click **Submit**.

■ The answer: Do you qualify?

9 If you want to proceed to actually apply for a mortgage, scroll down and click **Preapprove**. Then click **Apply/Secure Server**.

CONTINUED

PREQUALIFY AND APPLY
FOR A MORTGAGE ONLINE (CONTINUED)

You can fill out some forms online when you apply for a mortgage, but ultimately—with any mortgage site—you need some old-fashioned paper documentation of your income and credit history.

APPLY FOR A MORTGAGE

10 Fill in the standard information (name, Social Security number, and so on).

11 Authorize access to your credit report and click **Continue**.

12 Double-check the information.

13 Scroll down.

How much can I afford to pay for a house?

Mortgage lenders use a formula called 28/33: You should spend no more than 28 percent of your gross monthly income on your mortgage, or no more than 33 percent on your mortgage plus all other debts. To look at it another way: You can probably qualify for a mortgage that's three times your gross yearly income.

14 Fill in the requested information about the home you are buying, your sources of income, your employment, your educational background, and the real estate broker you used.

15 Click **Continue**.

16 Fill in the requested information about your current housing costs, assets, and liabilities.

17 On the next few pages, fill in information about your bank accounts, other assets, debts, and so on.

18 Click **Submit Application**.

CHAPTER 8

Other Online Investing

What kinds of investments can you buy besides the standard stocks, bonds, mutual funds, and real estate? Should you purchase a painting or an antique without seeing it in person? This chapter shows you how to buy and sell some alternative investments online.

DISTINGUISH BETWEEN VARIOUS TYPES OF INVESTMENTS

If *investing* means taking a stake in something that you expect to increase in value, then plenty of things can be called investments. After all, some people have discovered that the baseball cards they collected as kids are worth a small fortune years later.

DIVERSIFICATION

One advantage of so-called alternative investments is that they help you diversify your risk.

Generally, alternative investments do better when traditional securities, such as stocks, are not doing well, and vice versa. That is usually because of their relationship to inflation: Alternatives increase in value when inflation rises. By contrast, high inflation typically decreases the value of stocks and bonds.

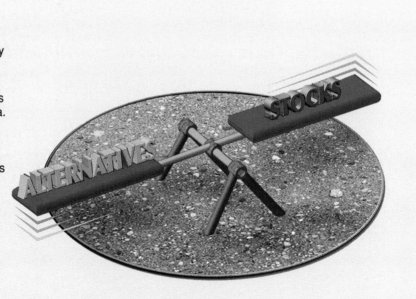

TYPES OF ALTERNATIVE INVESTMENTS

ART AND COLLECTIBLES

Of course, people purchase paintings, sculptures, and antiques because they enjoy looking at beautiful objects. But buyers of art are not exactly ignorant of the value of their acquisitions. If the object has some certification of authenticity, the owner can reasonably expect the value to go up.

You hear all the time about artwork being sold for very impressive amounts. For a sample, just go to an auction at one of the elite auction houses.

PRECIOUS METALS

Traditionally, investors have bought gold as a hedge— or protection—against inflation. The most common way to do this is to purchase gold coins from South Africa.

Starting around 1980, gold began to lose its allure to investors, mainly because inflation weakened and more types of investments flooded the scene. But a dedicated group of believers insists that gold is and always has been the only sure thing. This group maintains that when inflation roars again and the dollar weakens, the world will turn to gold, as it traditionally has, as the basis for international trade.

INSURANCE

The main purpose of insurance, of course, is to provide protection in case of a catastrophe. But you can use a whole-life insurance policy for both investment and insurance coverage.

A *whole-life policy* works like a savings account: You pay a premium to buy the insurance policy, and the insurance company guarantees you a minimum return on the cash value of the policy. For its part, the insurance company then invests your premium, just as a bank invests the money you deposit, hoping to make more than it will have to pay you.

You should only buy these policies, however, if you need long-term insurance to begin with.

BROWSE THE MARKET FOR ART AND COLLECTIBLES

A number of Web sites now sell fine artwork. This chapter uses eBay (www.ebay.com) as an example—even though it doesn't specialize in art—because it is one of the pioneers in online auctioneering. Also, eBay has a new Great Collections link with nine auction houses.

If you're thinking of investing in art or collectibles, I recommend focusing on pieces you like, not just on the potential returns. This is artwork, after all, not stock certificates. Why not display them on your walls and enjoy them until you're ready to sell? Besides, the more you enjoy putting together your collection, the more you'll learn about the art of that period, which will make you a more savvy investor.

BROWSE THE MARKET FOR ART AND COLLECTIBLES

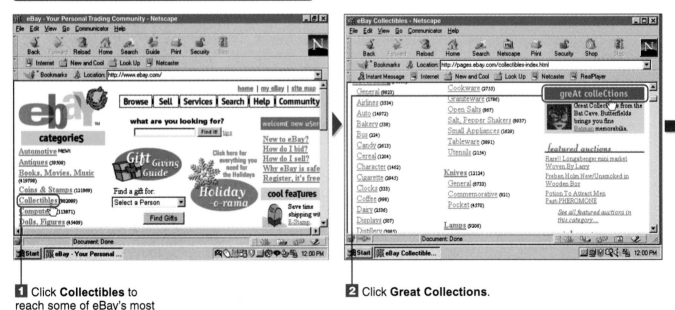

1 Click **Collectibles** to reach some of eBay's most valuable offerings.

2 Click **Great Collections**.

Can I really buy quality works of art online?

How about Henri de Toulouse-Lautrec, Gustav Klimt, Jim Dine, and Andy Warhol? Original pieces by all these artists have been offered on Artnet.com, eBay, and other online sites.

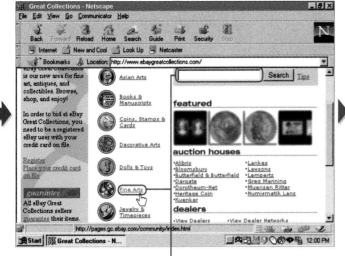

3 Click the type of artwork you want (**Fine Arts**, for example) OR type a description in the box next to Search.

■ If you choose Fine Arts from the Categories list on the Great Collections page, you reach the options on this page.

4 Click the category you are interested in to get more samples OR click the name of the particular artwork you are interested in at the bottom of this page to get more details.

REGISTER FOR ONLINE AUCTIONS

Naturally, online auction sites, such as eBay, need a record of who is buying and selling and how to contact him or her, so before you can bid for anything on these sites, you must register.

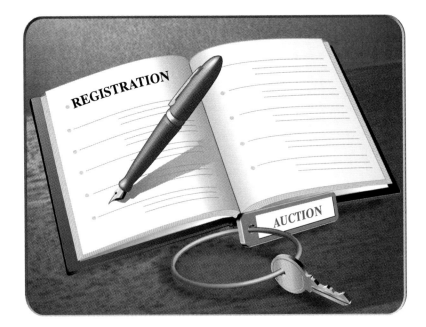

REGISTER FOR ONLINE AUCTIONS

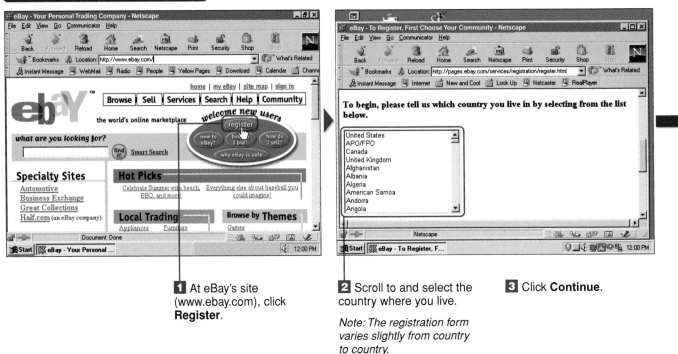

1 At eBay's site (www.ebay.com), click **Register**.

2 Scroll to and select the country where you live.

Note: The registration form varies slightly from country to country.

3 Click **Continue**.

Can anyone register?

You must be at least 18 years old. That's because minors can't sign contracts, and a winning auction bid is a legal contract.

4 Fill in your name, e-mail address, street address, and phone number.

5 Scroll down.

6 If you want, fill in the optional information such as the areas you are most interested in, your age, and how you learned about eBay.

CONTINUED

You can stay anonymous while you bid on eBay by making up a user ID (although other eBay users will be able to request your e-mail address). But if your bid wins, you and the seller have to contact each other.

REGISTER FOR ONLINE AUCTIONS (CONTINUED)

7 Click **Continue**.

8 Review your information and click **Continue**.

? Do I have to put down any sort of down payment?

No. Registering as a buyer on eBay's site is free. But to bid on the site's Great Collections artwork, you will have to provide credit card information.

9 Review the user agreement, check the required check boxes (☐ changes to ☑), and click **I Accept This Agreement**.

■ You may have to wait 24 hours to get your confirmation code via e-mail. Often, though, eBay e-mails you the code within the hour.

10 After you receive your confirmation code e-mail, log on to eBay again to confirm your registration.

11 Fill in your e-mail address and confirmation code.

12 Create a new password.

13 Choose a user ID, if you want to use one.

BUY ARTWORK ONLINE

Online art sites are run by galleries, by elite auction houses such as Sotheby's, and by new ventures formed just for this purpose.

Gallery Auction

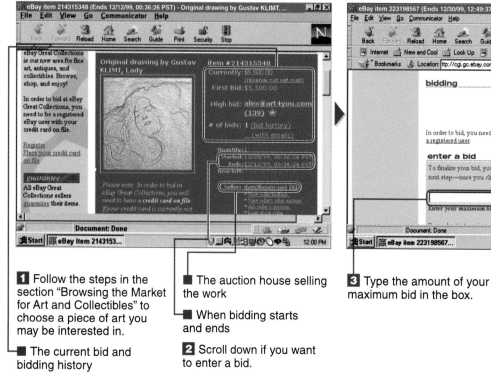

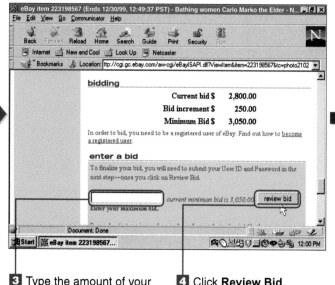

1 Follow the steps in the section "Browsing the Market for Art and Collectibles" to choose a piece of art you may be interested in.

■ The current bid and bidding history

■ The auction house selling the work

■ When bidding starts and ends

2 Scroll down if you want to enter a bid.

3 Type the amount of your maximum bid in the box.

4 Click **Review Bid**.

5 On the next screen that appears, scroll down and click **View Comments About Your Seller** to see what other buyers have said about the seller.

?

What if the painting I buy does not look like what I expected based on the on-screen photo?

No problem. Online art dealers typically guarantee that you can return a purchase within a set period of time if it differs markedly from the description or if it is damaged.

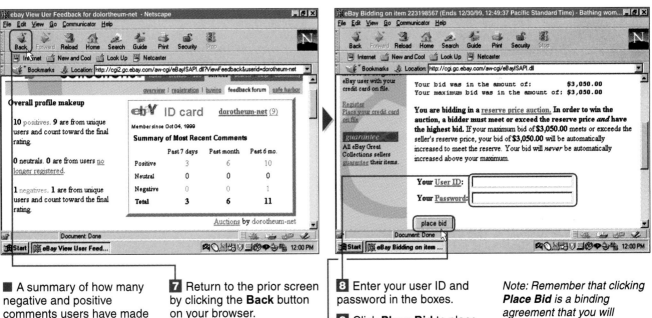

■ A summary of how many negative and positive comments users have made about the seller

6 Scroll down for more detailed comments about the seller.

7 Return to the prior screen by clicking the **Back** button on your browser.

8 Enter your user ID and password in the boxes.

9 Click **Place Bid** to place your bid.

*Note: Remember that clicking **Place Bid** is a binding agreement that you will purchase the item if you are the highest bidder. You can retract a bid only in a few, very rare circumstances.*

CHECK OUT GOLD AND PRECIOUS METAL PRICES

Until 1971, every U.S. dollar was backed by a dollar's worth of gold, and some investors think that the metal will play an important role again one day. You can look up gold prices at the Goldsheet Mining Directory Web site (www.Goldsheet. simplenet.com).

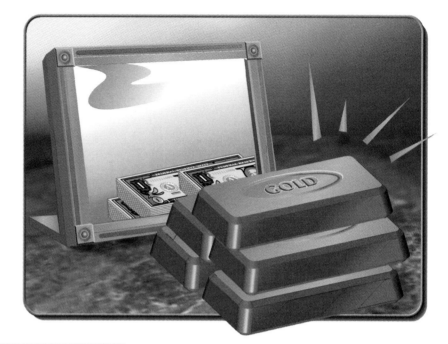

CHECK OUT GOLD AND PRECIOUS METAL PRICES

1 Click **Quotes**.

2 Scroll down and click **Gold, Silver, and Platinum Prices**, from Chamber of Mines of South Africa.

Can I just walk into a store and buy gold?

Probably the easiest way to own gold is to buy South African Krugerrands (gold coins) through a dealer. You can buy gold jewelry, too, but then you also have to judge the value of the craftsmanship.

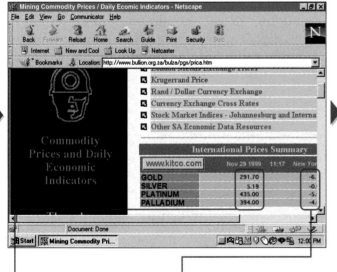

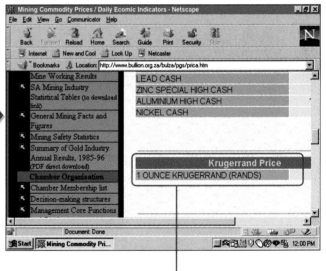

■ Current prices of gold, silver, platinum, and palladium.

■ How much the price has gone up or down.

3 Scroll down for prices of other metals and Krugerrand coins.

■ Price of Krugerrand gold coins.

RESEARCH INSURANCE ONLINE

The Internet is a convenient way to compare premium prices for most insurance policies. One good source is Quotesmith.com (www.quotesmith.com), which gathers quotes from more than 300 insurance companies.

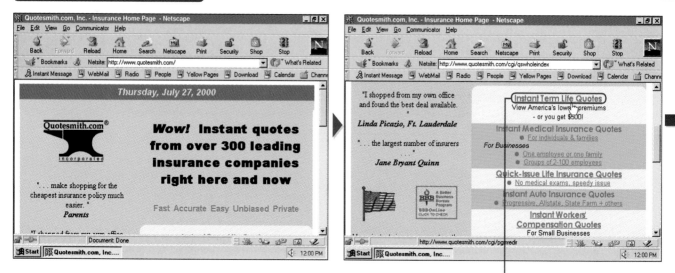

1 Scroll down to select from a choice of types of insurance.

2 Click **Instant Term Life Quotes**.

? Can I do the whole process online?

No, some things still need the direct human touch. The insurance company may want to check your credit record or driving history or put you through a medical checkup.

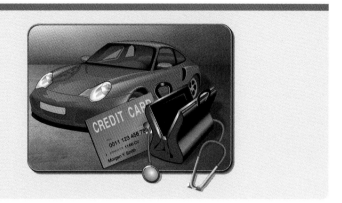

3 Fill in the requested, basic information (birth date, state of residence, sex, tobacco use, coverage amount, and so on).

4 Scroll down and click **View Instant Quotes**.

■ The company's rating from A.M. Best Co.

Note: A.M. Best rates insurance companies from A++ (superior) all the way down to F (in liquidation) and S (rating suspended).

■ The cost for the first year.

CHAPTER 9

Banking Online

How much of your ordinary banking needs can you take care of via the Internet? What if you need to correct a mistake? This chapter shows you how to pay bills, apply for a credit card, stop payment on a check, and handle other banking tasks online.

UNDERSTAND HOW BANK ACCOUNTS WORK

The safest thing you can do with your money is to put it into a bank account. The Federal Deposit Insurance Corporation (FDIC), a U.S. government agency, insures bank deposits of up to $100,000.

REMEMBERING RISK AND RETURN

Because the risks of putting your money in a bank account are so low, the returns are also relatively low. In fact, you may not ordinarily think of a bank account as an investment. After all, you are not really putting your assets at risk or taking a stake in a venture. You are just putting money away for safekeeping—that is, saving, not investing.

But some bank accounts enable you to make more money off your deposited money. So you may think of them as a very secure, very simple way of starting to invest.

With banking, you can add another rule of risk and return: The easier it is to take your money out, the lower the returns.

DISTINGUISH BETWEEN DIFFERENT TYPES OF BANK ACCOUNTS

CHECKING ACCOUNT

A checking account is the least likely to be seen as an investment or savings vehicle. A *checking account* is essentially a kind of parking place that keeps your money safe until you need it. You can easily take cash out whenever you want—by writing a check, by using an ATM machine, or by going to a bank teller in person.

Checking accounts pay little or no interest. They may also charge fees and require a minimum balance. The two basic types of fees are monthly fees and fees for each withdrawal or check.

SAVINGS ACCOUNT

A *savings account* combines the advantages of investing (offering you a moderate interest income) and a checking account (giving you fairly easy accessibility to your cash).

Savings accounts pay higher interest than checking accounts but let you get your money out almost as easily. Depending on the exact terms of the account, you can typically withdraw your money just about any time by going in person to a bank teller or through an ATM.

However, the point of this kind of account is supposed to be to save the money, not withdraw it!

CERTIFICATE OF DEPOSIT

Because *Certificates of Deposit* (CDs) pay the highest rate of return of any bank account, they naturally have the most restrictions. The money must stay in the account for a set period of time—usually, from six months to two years. If you withdraw any of it early, you pay a penalty.

DECIDE TO BANK ONLINE

Maybe you like getting writer's cramp, scribbling out names and numbers on your checks when you pay your bills every month. And maybe you like standing in line at the teller's window or the ATM to find out your bank balance. But if you find those chores a little tiring, you could try online banking.

Of course, you can't get cash or make deposits online, although you can make electronic transfers.

SAVING TIME AND MONEY

When you bank online, you can find out whether a check has cleared or how much money is available in your account with only a few clicks of your mouse and keyboard. Similarly, you can easily transfer money between accounts.

Best of all, you can pay bills online. You can set up a system that automatically pays your regular bills—such as your car loan, student loan, mortgage, or rent—and then, if you wish, completely ignore this paperless paperwork. You can also pay occasional bills online or even send someone an electronic check as a birthday present. And do not forget the money you save on postage!

PROTECTING YOUR MONEY

But what if you need to call a halt to one of your automated electronic processes? For example, you may have been charged for a credit card purchase you never made. Will your account automatically spew out the money to pay the incorrect bill?

Even problems like these can be handled online. You can stop payment on a check, question a charge, or arrange credit. Also, for most of your online bill-paying, you will have to specifically authorize the payments, so you have plenty of chances to stop any money from going out.

Chapter 11 discusses some concerns you may have about privacy and security when sending sensitive financial information over the Internet.

GETTING HUMAN HELP

Banking online does not have to mean being locked up in solitary confinement with your computer. If you have a question about how to proceed or if something seems to be going wrong, all online systems have a Help key that gives you answers on-screen to common questions. And often, you can phone customer service or a help desk for more personal assistance.

OPEN AN ONLINE ACCOUNT AND SIGN ON

All the major banks in the United States—and plenty of smaller ones, too—offer online banking. Some banks, in fact, exist only in cyberspace and have no actual branches for you to visit.

This chapter uses Citibank's demonstration program as an example because Citibank is the largest bank in the United States. This section shows you how to set up a test account, using the demo program. The steps are very similar for an actual account at Citibank, but of course, other banks' online programs may work differently.

OPEN AN ONLINE ACCOUNT AND SIGN ON

1 At Citibank's home page (www.citibank.com), select your country. From the list of products and services, select **Direct Access** under **Online Banking**.

2 If you want to follow the demo program, click **Test**

Drive; then click **Start Test Drive**, **Enter**, **Screen Reader**, and **Customer Service**.

■ OR, if you want to open an actual Citibank account, from the Direct Access screen, click **Open an Account** (and skip step 3).

3 Click **Open an Account**.

4 Click the type of account you want to open (such as **Open a Checking Account**).

What if I need help?

You can talk to a live human being in customer service via a toll-free phone number. Citibank's number is listed on the Welcome page of its online banking site (1-800-374-9700 at the time of this book's writing), and service reps are on call 24 hours a day. Citibank encourages users to call customer service to correct wrong names or addresses.

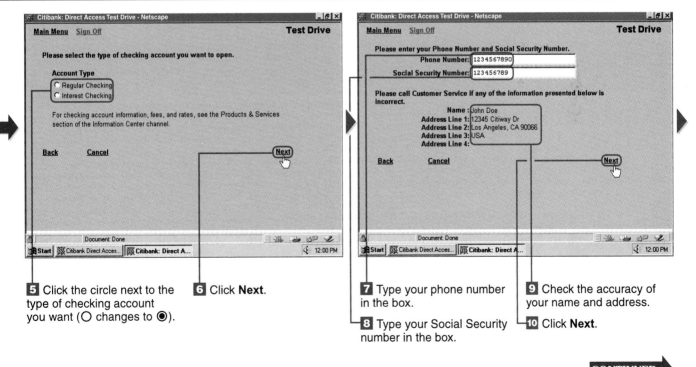

5 Click the circle next to the type of checking account you want (○ changes to ◉).

6 Click **Next**.

7 Type your phone number in the box.

8 Type your Social Security number in the box.

9 Check the accuracy of your name and address.

10 Click **Next**.

CONTINUED

Online banking does not have to be a race. You go through many deliberate steps before you actually open an account.

OPEN AN ONLINE ACCOUNT AND SIGN ON (CONTINUED)

11 Scroll down the list of your bank accounts and click the one from which you will withdraw money to start this new account.

12 Type the dollar amount you want to open the account with in the white box.

Note: You do not need to type a $.

13 Click **Next**.

14 Click the circle next to the type of account you are opening (O changes to ⊙). (If this is a standard individual or joint account for yourself, click **Not a Trust**.)

Note: A trust account means it is really someone else's money —

quite often, a child's — which you are taking care of temporarily.

15 Click **Next**.

How do I find out what types of accounts the bank has and the rules for each?

You don't need to leave the computer. Look under "Products and Services" on the bank's Web site.

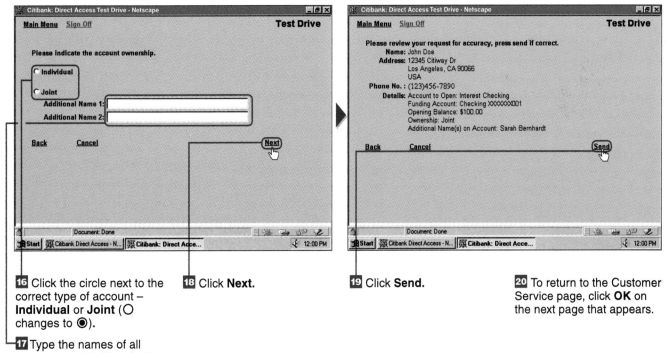

16 Click the circle next to the correct type of account – **Individual** or **Joint** (○ changes to ◉).

17 Type the names of all other account holders in the boxes, if it is a joint account.

18 Click **Next**.

19 Click **Send**.

20 To return to the Customer Service page, click **OK** on the next page that appears.

FIND OUT YOUR ACCOUNT BALANCE

With an online bank account, your account information may not be quite up-to-the-minute, but it will be no more than a day off: You may miss deposits or withdrawals that were made after the close of business on the day you log on.

FIND OUT YOUR ACCOUNT BALANCE

1 Log on to your online account if you have one (and if it's a Citibank account, go to the Direct Access Account Information page). If you want to just follow a demo, follow steps 1 and 2 in the section "Opening an Online Account and Signing On," but instead of clicking **Customer Service**, click **Account Information**.

2 Click **See Account Information**.

3 Click any account.

Is there another way to find out my balance?

Yes, when you transfer money between accounts in the Citibank system, you also get a current reading of the balance in those two accounts.

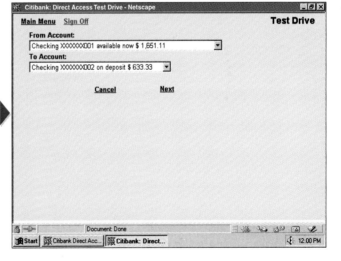

4 Scroll through the options under **Select the Value to Sort By** if you want to change the way the information is displayed (by date, by dollar value, and so on).

5 Scroll down under **Select the Order** to arrange whether to display checks by increasing or decreasing value.

*Note: This is how account balances are displayed if you get the information the alternative way, by transferring money. To do so, on the main Direct Access menu, click **Payments and Transfers**. On the next page, click **Make a Transfer**.*

TRANSFER MONEY BETWEEN ACCOUNTS

Because you can know exactly how much is in all your accounts at virtually any given moment, you can plan your budget precisely. You can transfer your funds online between accounts exactly when you want to, leaving cash in a higher-interest-bearing account until you actually need it in a checking account to pay bills.

TRANSFER MONEY BETWEEN ACCOUNTS

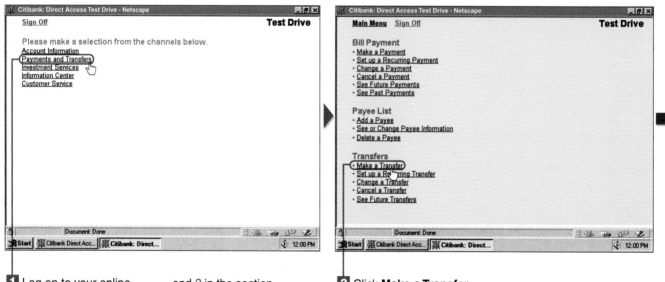

1 Log on to your online account if you have one (and if it's a Citibank account, go to the Direct Access Payments and Transfers page). If you want to just follow a demo, follow steps 1 and 2 in the section "Opening an Online Account and Signing On," but instead of clicking **Customer Service,** click **Payments and Transfers**.

2 Click **Make a Transfer**.

190

Can I really wait until the last minute to transfer money?

You should give yourself some breathing room—say, at least one day before you need the money. What if you have computer problems, or you get sick?

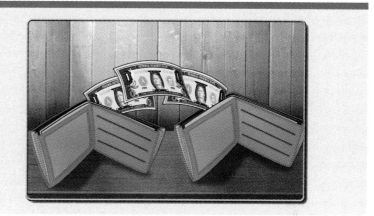

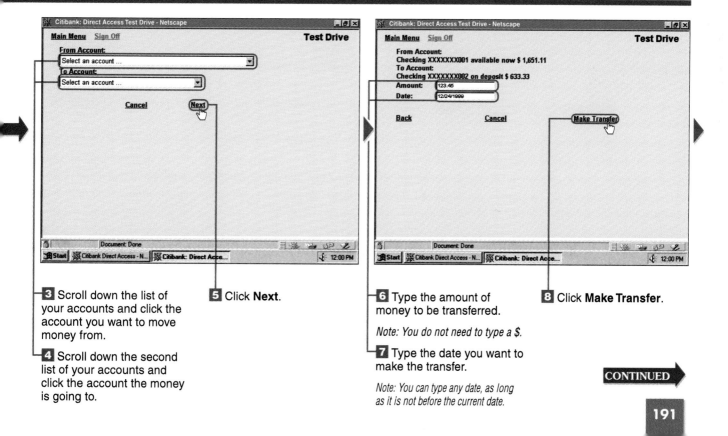

3 Scroll down the list of your accounts and click the account you want to move money from.

4 Scroll down the second list of your accounts and click the account the money is going to.

5 Click **Next**.

6 Type the amount of money to be transferred.

Note: You do not need to type a $.

7 Type the date you want to make the transfer.

Note: You can type any date, as long as it is not before the current date.

8 Click **Make Transfer**.

CONTINUED

TRANSFER MONEY BETWEEN ACCOUNTS (CONTINUED)

As you reach the final steps, you get several chances to change your mind.

TRANSFER MONEY BETWEEN ACCOUNTS (CONTINUED)

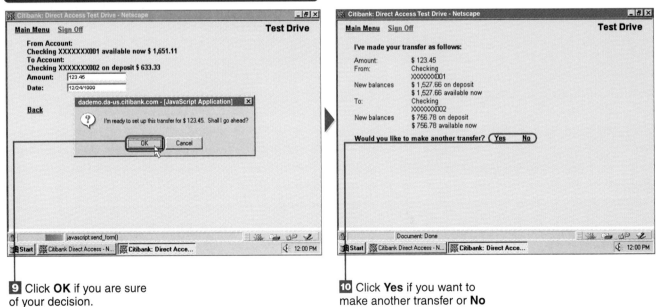

9 Click **OK** if you are sure of your decision.

10 Click **Yes** if you want to make another transfer or **No** if you don't.

Can I change my mind about transferring money?

As long as money has not been moved, you can halt a transfer you scheduled.

CHANGE OR CANCEL A TRANSFER

	Citibank: Direct Access Test Drive - Netscape			
Main Menu **Sign Off**				**Test Drive**

Here are your future transfers. Please click one to change.

Date	From Account	To Account	Reference Number	Amount
01/01/2000	Checking XXXXXXX001	Gold AAdvantage Visa XXXXXXXXXXXX122	10133	$ 1,977.69
01/15/2000	Checking XXXXXXX002	Citibank MasterCard XXXXXXXXXXXX073	10134	$ 89.83
01/20/2000	Day-to-Day Savings XXXXXXX002	Checking XXXXXXX001	not available	$ 500.00

Back

Document: Done

Start | Citibank Direct Access - N... | Citibank: Direct Acce... | 12:00 PM

	Citibank: Direct Access Test Drive - Netscape			
Main Menu **Sign Off**				**Test Drive**

Please modify the transfer details and click **Change Transfer**.

From Account:
Checking XXXXXXX001 available now $ 1,527.66

To Account:
Gold AAdvantage Visa

Date: 01/01/2000

Amount:
- Current Transfer Amount $ 1,977.69
- Balance Due on Last Statement as of 11/14/1999 $ 1,977.69
- Minimum Payment due by 12/22/1999 $ 120.00
- Current Unpaid Balance: $ 3,198.91
- Another Amount

Back   **Change Transfer**

Document: Done

Start | Citibank Direct Access - N... | Citibank: Direct Acce... | 12:00 PM

---

1 Return to the Direct Access main menu and click **Payments and Transfers**. On the next page, click **Change a Transfer** (or **Cancel a Transfer**).

2 Click an account in the To Account column in order to block funds from going there.

3 Type the new date in the box, if that's what you want to change.

4 Type the new amount in the box, if that's what you want to change.

5 Make any other changes you want.

6 Click **Change Transfer**.

STOP PAYMENT ON A CHECK

Although banking online can make a lot of financial chores easier, it cannot eliminate all mistakes. So you can also fix mistakes on the Net. For example, you can stop payment on checks when necessary.

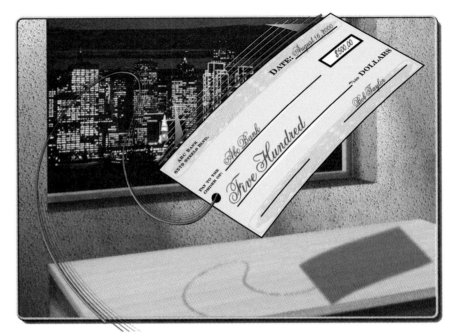

1 Log on to your account (with a Citibank account, go to the Stop Payment of a Check page). If you want to use a demo, follow steps 1 and 2 in "Opening an Online Account and Signing On." Click **Stop Payment of a Check**.

2 Scroll down and select the account.

3 Type the check number.

4 Fill in the **Date**, **Payee Name**, **Amount**, and **Explanation** fields.

5 Click **Next**.

6 Type your phone number in the white box.

7 Click **Next**.

Do I need a good reason to stop payment?

A simple "bill was incorrect" will suffice in the Citibank program.

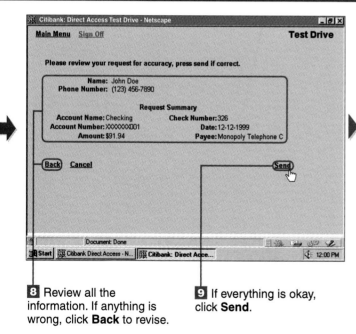

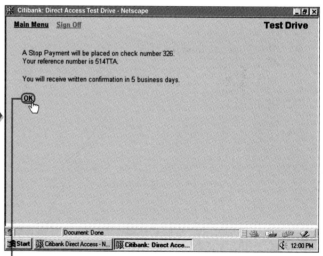

8 Review all the information. If anything is wrong, click **Back** to revise.

9 If everything is okay, click **Send**.

10 Click **OK**.

Note: For its final confirmation, Citibank relies on paper!

SET UP AUTOMATIC PAYMENTS FOR RECURRING BILLS

It's easy to have your bank automatically pay recurring bills for which the amount of payment never changes, such as a mortgage.

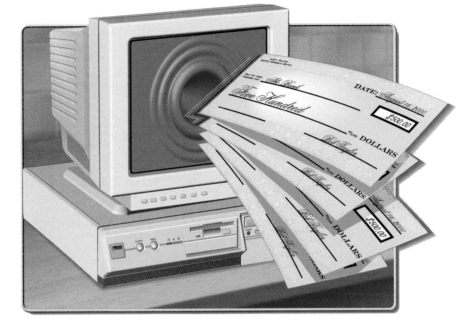

1 Log on to your online account if you have one (and if it's a Citibank account, go to the Direct Access Set up a Recurring Payment page). If you want to just follow a demo, follow steps 1 and 2

in the section "Opening an Online Account and Signing On," but instead of clicking **Customer Service**, click **Payments and Transfers** and then click **Set up a Recurring Payment**.

2 Click the name of the payee.

3 Scroll down to select the bank account you want to pay from and click the account.

4 Type in the amount to be paid.

5 Scroll down and select the payment frequency (weekly, monthly, and so on).

6 Click next to the circle that indicates when payments will stop (O changes to ◉).

7 Click **Set Up Payment**.

What if I change my mind about a payment?

At any time, you can go online to change or cancel any future payments, as shown in the sections "Change a Payment" and "Cancel a Payment" later in this chapter.

Void

Enter the information for your payment.
As a reminder, it is best to schedule your payment 5 to 7 business days before its due date.

Payee: VRA CAR LOAN Account #: AL963250f982
Last Payment Date: 08/15/1999 Amount: $ 150.16

From Account: Checking XXXXXXX001 available now $ 1,527.66

I'm ready to set up this payment for $150.16 to continue until the total amount of $10,000.00 is reached. Shall I go ahead?

OK   Cancel

Memo to Payee: KIDS CAR LOAN

Back   Cancel   Set Up Payment

I've scheduled your payment as follows:

Amount: $ 150.16 to be sent by check
From: Checking XXXXXXX001
To: VRA CAR LOAN AL963250f982
First payment date: 12/25/1999
Payment frequency: Monthly
Total payments: 67
Total amount: $ 10,000.00
Memo to payee: KIDS CAR LOAN

Would you like to make another payment? Yes   No

8 Click **OK**.

Note: This is another chance to change your mind.

■ Your final confirmation.

PAY ONE-TIME BILLS AND RECURRING BILLS THAT VARY

You can pay almost any bill electronically—including bills whose amounts vary from month to month, such as your phone or electric bill. You can even send out one-time checks, such as birthday gifts! Citibank's program has you arrange electronic payment for these bills in two steps: First, you add the vendor as a regular payee. Then, before each bill is due, you authorize the bank to make the payment.

ADD A PAYEE

ADDING A NEW PAYEE

1 Log on to your online account (with a Citibank account, go to the Add a Payee page). If you want to just use a demo, follow steps 1 and 2 in the section

"Opening an Online Account and Signing On," but instead of clicking **Customer Service**, click **Payments and Transfers**. Then click **Add a Payee**.

2 Type in the vendor's name.

3 Click **Next**.

4 On the next page, click **A Different Payee.**

5 On the next page, type in the vendor's address, the account number you want to pay from, and anything you want to say in the memo.

6 Click **Add Payee**.

198

What if I never need to pay the same vendor again?

No problem. Unless you go online and tell the bank to make a payment, no money will ever be sent.

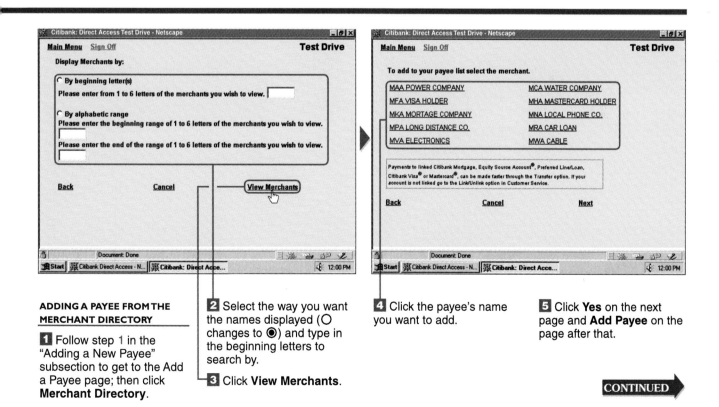

ADDING A PAYEE FROM THE MERCHANT DIRECTORY

1 Follow step 1 in the "Adding a New Payee" subsection to get to the Add a Payee page; then click **Merchant Directory**.

2 Select the way you want the names displayed (○ changes to ●) and type in the beginning letters to search by.

3 Click **View Merchants**.

4 Click the payee's name you want to add.

5 Click **Yes** on the next page and **Add Payee** on the page after that.

CONTINUED

Varying and one-time bills require a little more work than the recurring type. Still, all you have to do is type in the amount to be paid. The bank does everything else.

MAKE PAYMENTS

1 To make a payment, first follow the procedure to add a payee outlined in the subsection "Adding a Payee." Then return to the Payment and Transfers dialog box and select **Make a Payment**.

2 Click the name of the payee.

3 Scroll down and select the account you want to pay from.

4 Type the amount to be paid and the date you want it to be paid.

5 Click **Make Payment**.

What if I switch vendors?

You can delete this vendor and add the new one. Then you can continue making payments the same way.

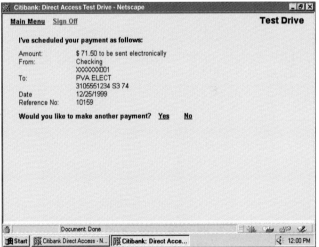

6 Click **OK**.

Note: This is another chance to change your mind.

■ Your final confirmation.

DELETE A PAYEE

For a number of reasons, you may no longer want your bank to pay a particular utility, merchant, mortgage lender, or other company. You may trade in your car and pay off the car loan, for example. In cases such as these, you can delete the payee to make sure it isn't paid accidentally.

DELETE A PAYEE

1 Log on to your online account if you have one (and if it's a Citibank account, go to the Direct Access Delete a Payee page). If you want to just follow a demo, follow steps 1 and 2 in the section

"Opening an Online Account and Signing On," but instead of clicking **Customer Service**, click **Payments and Transfers**. Then click **Delete a Payee**.

2 Click the payee's name.

3 Click **Yes**.

Why should I save the payment summary?

The interest you paid may well be tax-deductible. Even if you are no longer paying the bills now, you need proof of past payments when you do your taxes.

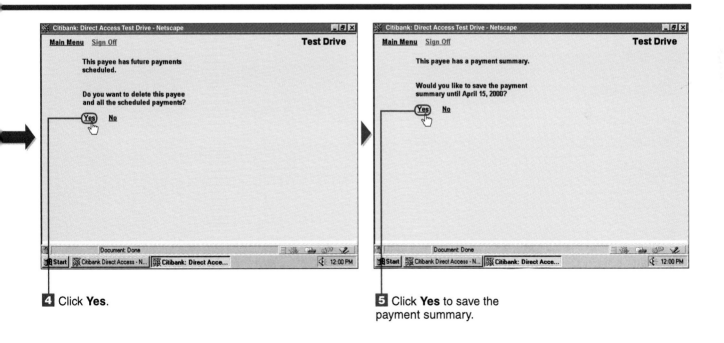

4 Click **Yes**.

5 Click **Yes** to save the payment summary.

CHANGE A PAYMENT

You are not permanently chained to any of the parts of your automatic bill-paying arrangement. You can change payments whenever you need to. If you are low on cash this month in the checking account you usually use, you can arrange to make the next payment from another account.

CHANGE A PAYMENT

1 Log on to your online account if you have one (and if it's a Citibank account, go to the Payments and Transfers page). If you want to just follow a demo, follow steps 1 and 2 in the section

"Opening an Online Account and Signing On," but instead of clicking **Customer Service**, click **Payments and Transfers**.

2 Click **Change a Payment**.

3 Click the payment you want to change.

204

How many aspects of a payment can I change at once?

You can change the amount you pay and the account you pay from in one movement in Citibank's program. To switch the company you pay, see the sections "Delete a Payee" and "Pay One-Time Bills and Recurring Bills That Vary."

Citibank: Direct Access Test Drive - Netscape

Main Menu   Sign Off   **Test Drive**

Please modify the payment details and click **Change Payment**.
As a reminder, it is best to schedule your payment 5 to 7 business days before its due date.

Payee:	**CKA MORTAGE**
From Account:	Checking XXXXXXX002 available now $ 756.78
Amount:	$ 18.44 paid electronically
Date:	01/10/2000

Back   (**Change Payment**)

Document: Done

Start   Citibank Direct Access - N...   Citibank: Direct Acce...   12:00 PM

Citibank: Direct Access Test Drive - Netscape

Main Menu   Sign Off   **Test Drive**

I've changed your payment as follows:

Amount:	$ 18.44 to be sent electronically
From:	Checking
	XXXXXXX001
To:	CKA MORTAGE
Date	01/10/2000
Reference No:	10147

Would you like to change another payment? **Yes   No**

Document: Done

Start   Citibank Direct Access - N...   Citibank: Direct Acce...   12:00 PM

---

4 Scroll down to the account you want to take money from and click (if that is what you want to change).

5 Type in the new amount you want to pay (if that is what you want to change).

6 Click **Change Payment**.

7 Click **OK** in the confirmation dialog box.

■ This confirms your action.

CANCEL A PAYMENT

On rare occasions, you may want to skip one particular payment—say, if you made a double payment the month before. For a situation like this, you can cancel a payment.

CANCEL A PAYMENT

Here are your future payments. Select one to cancel.

Back

Date	Payee	Payment Method	Reference Number	Amount
01/01/2000	PVA ELECT	Electronic	10135	$ 127.02
01/05/2000	ONA L PHONE	Electronic	10136	$ 89.20
01/05/2000	2FA VISA	Electronic	10137	$ 104.34
01/06/2000	0AA POWER	Electronic	10138	$ 97.45
01/07/2000	DFA VISA	Electronic	10139	$ 134.78
01/07/2000	GVA ELECT	Check	not available	$ 22.50
01/10/2000	NCA WATER	Electronic	10141	$ 48.31
01/10/2000	CKA MORTAGE	Electronic	10142	$ 18.44

Here are the payment details.

Amount: $ 18.44 to be sent electronically
From: Checking
XXXXXXX002
To: CKA MORTAGE
Date: 01/10/2000

Would you like to cancel this payment? Yes No

1 Log on to your online account (and if it's a Citibank account, go to the Cancel a Payment page). If you want to just follow a demo, follow steps 1 and 2 in the section "Opening an Online Account and Signing On," but instead of clicking **Customer Service**, click **Payments and Transfers**. Then click **Cancel a Payment**.

2 Click the payment you want to cancel.

3 Click **Yes**.

VIEW YOUR BILL PAYMENT RECORD

In order to have a complete record, you need to see all your payments, whether they were made by check or online. Luckily, the bank can do that.

VIEW YOUR BILL PAYMENT RECORD

Citibank: Direct Access Test Drive - Netscape

Main Menu   Sign Off   **Test Drive**

Select a payee to view past payments by specific payee or click <u>View all Payments</u> to see all past payments.

OAA POWER	AVA ELECT	BPA LONGDIST
DFA VISA	FHA MSTERCRD	GVA ELECT
IRA CAR LOAN	JWA CABLE	KHA MSTERCRD
MFA VISA	NCA WATER	ONA L PHONE
PVA ELECT	RFA VISA	SPA LONGDIST
VRA CAR LOAN	YHA MSTERCRD	

View all Payments

Document: Done

Start | Citibank Direct Access - N... | Citibank: Direct Acce... | 12:00 PM

Citibank: Direct Access Test Drive - Netscape

Main Menu   Sign Off   **Test Drive**

Here are your past payments.

Back

Date	Payee	Payment Method	Reference Number	Amount	Status
11/29/1999	WA CABLE	Check	10132	$ 10.00	Open
11/26/1999	ONA L PHONE	Check	10131	$ 124.74	Open
11/24/1999	PVA ELECT	Electronic	10130	$ 164.35	Closed
11/22/1999	RFA VISA	Check	10129	$ 51.43	Closed
11/18/1999	SPA LONGDIST	Electronic	10128	$ 145.43	Closed
11/12/1999	VRA CAR LOAN	Electronic	10126	$ 124.45	Closed
11/10/1999	YHA MSTERCRD	Electronic	10125	$ 46.35	Closed
11/10/1999	ARA CAR LOAN	Electronic	10124	$ 12.63	Closed

Document: Done

Start | Citibank Direct Access - N... | Citibank: Direct Acce... | 12:00 PM

1 Log on to your online account if you have one (and if it's a Citibank account, go to the Direct Access See Past Payments page). If you want to just follow a demo, follow steps 1 and 2 in the section "Opening an Online Account and Signing On," but instead of clicking **Customer Service**, click **Payments and Transfers**. Then click **See Past Payments**.

2 Click a name or click **View All Payments**.

3 Check through your payments.

FIX A PROBLEM WITH A BILL

Even with the most careful customer in the world, mistakes still occur. Correcting problems that already happened is a little harder than canceling future payments, but you can do it.

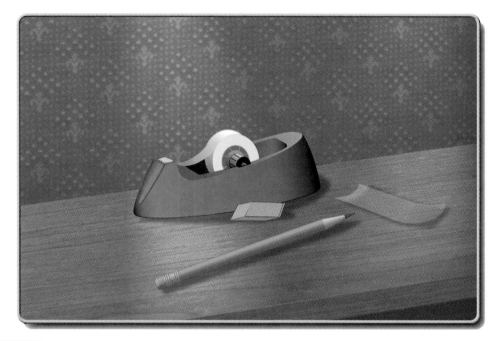

FIX A PROBLEM WITH A BILL

1 Log on to your online account if you have one (and if it's a Citibank account, go to the Direct Access Report a Bill Payment Problem page). If you want to just follow a demo, follow steps 1 and 2 in the section "Opening an Online Account and Signing On." On the next page, click **Report a Bill Payment Problem**.

2 Click the payee's name.

3 Click **Next**.

4 Scroll down to the check number and click it.

5 Click **Next**.

Can my problem be fixed online immediately?

No, even online banking is not that quick. You can explain the problem and ask for help. But the bank still needs time to investigate the issue.

6 Type a description of your problem in the box.

7 Click the box or boxes next to the action or actions you would like the bank to take, or type your request in the **Other Action Requested** box.

8 Click **Next**.

9 Check your request for accuracy and click **Send**.

APPLY FOR A CREDIT CARD

If you can shop online with a credit card, it is only fair that you should be able to obtain the card electronically, too.

You can apply for a credit card on many banks' Web sites. This section uses Citibank as an example; the steps will probably be similar for other banks' sites.

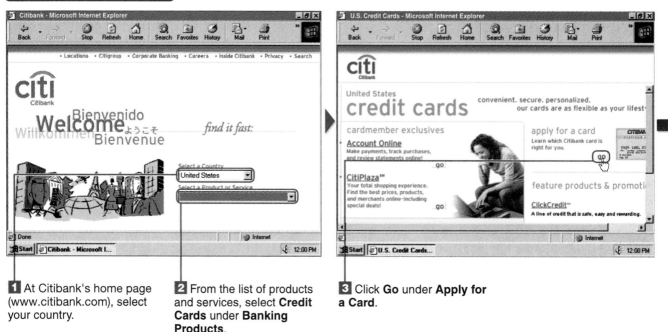

1 At Citibank's home page (www.citibank.com), select your country.

2 From the list of products and services, select **Credit Cards** under **Banking Products**.

3 Click **Go** under **Apply for a Card**.

What kind of information do I need to provide?

The online application form is just like a typical paper form. You need to provide basic personal information, such as the types of bank accounts you have, whether you rent or own your house, your gross household income, your address, your job title, and your mother's maiden name.

Credit Card
Application Form

Name:
Address:
Types of Bank Accounts:
Rent or Own Home:
Gross Household Income:
Job Title:
Mother's Maiden Name:

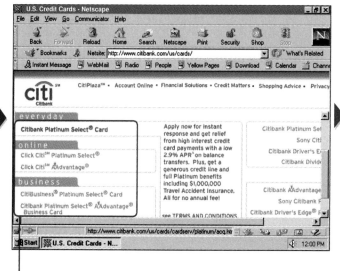

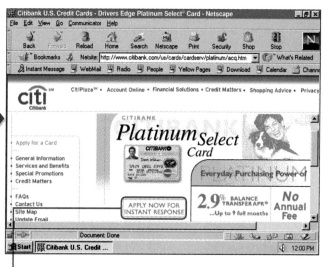

4 Click the type of card you want.

5 Click **Apply Now for Instant Response**.

6 On the next two pages, fill in all the fields of the online form and click **Continue**.

7 Fill in the fields on the next page, read through the terms and conditions, and click **Submit** if you accept them.

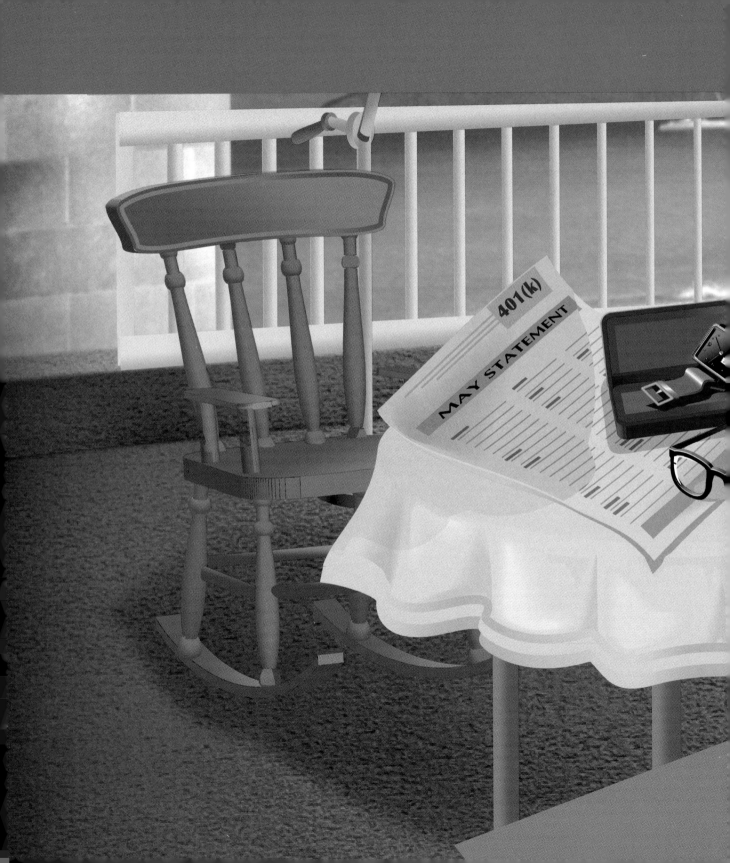

CHAPTER 10

Planning for Retirement Online

How much should you be saving for retirement? How much more will you have at age 65 if you increase the stock holdings in your 401(k) now? This chapter shows you some Web sites that can help you figure all this out.

PREPARE FOR RETIREMENT BY USING A TYPICAL ONLINE PLANNER

Retirement planning is one of the most popular services on the Internet, with special calculators available from many portals, mutual fund companies, brokerages, and even news organizations. This chapter shows you how to use two of the online retirement planners: Quicken.com, which is an example of a fairly typical planner, and Financial Engines, which takes an unusual approach to factoring in the unpredictable.

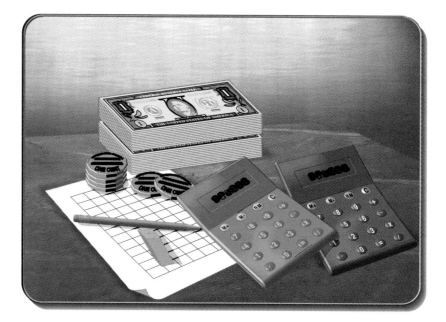

LOG ON TO QUICKEN.COM'S RETIREMENT PLANNER

1 At Quicken.com (www.quicken.com), click **Retirement**.

2 Click **Build a Retirement Plan**.

Note: You can also scroll down to Retirement QuickAnswers for more information on retirement issues.

How do I decide which retirement planner to use?

Use several. By comparing all the answers, you can end up with a pretty good range of possible retirement outcomes.

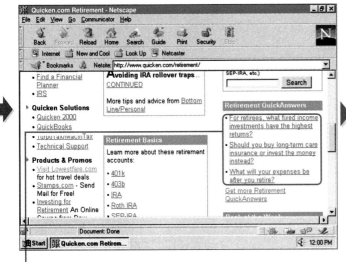

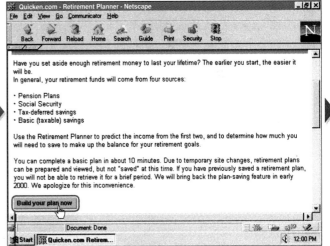

■ Instead of clicking Build a Retirement Plan, on the Retirement page you can click any question for more details about that aspect of retirement. If you do so, click **Back** and then **Build a Retirement Plan** to continue your retirement plan.

3 Click **Build Your Plan Now**.

CONTINUED

PREPARE FOR RETIREMENT BY USING A TYPICAL ONLINE PLANNER (CONTINUED)

Before you can figure out how much to save, you should take into account what you are starting with.

INPUT KEY INFORMATION ABOUT INCOME AND SAVINGS

4 Enter the requested information about you and your spouse: birth date, gender, desired retirement age, and whether or not you smoke.

5 Click **Estimate**.

■ Quicken estimates your and your spouse's life expectancy, based on your current age, gender, and smoking profile.

6 Click **Next**.

7 Enter the requested information about salary, expected raises, and the amount you will need to live on.

8 Click **Next**.

? How much income will I need after I retire?

Some of your expenses—such as commuting costs to work—will decline, but others—such as medical care—will probably increase. That is why experts suggest that you aim for 70 to 80 percent of your pre-retirement income.

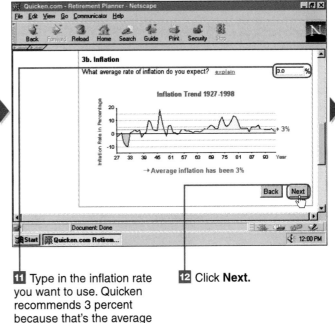

9 Click the arrow (▼) next to the list of states and scroll down until you hit the state where you live.

10 Click **Estimate Tax Rate.**

■ The correct tax rate for your state automatically appears in the boxes.

11 Type in the inflation rate you want to use. Quicken recommends 3 percent because that's the average for the late 1990s.

12 Click **Next.**

CONTINUED

PREPARE FOR RETIREMENT BY USING A TYPICAL ONLINE PLANNER (CONTINUED)

Every few years you should update your retirement calculations. All kinds of things in your life could change, such as your savings habits or your job.

INPUT KEY INFORMATION ABOUT INCOME AND SAVINGS (CONTINUED)

13 Enter the requested information about your and your spouse's 401(k), IRA, and Roth IRA plans.

14 Click **Next**.

15 Enter the amount of money you expect to get from Social Security.

Note: Just to prove that these calculators aren't without a sense of irony, the program allows you to leave the space blank if you have no faith in the Social Security system.

?

How can I learn how much is due to me from Social Security or my company pension?

You will have to request the information from the Social Security Administration and your employer's benefits office. It could take a few weeks.

---

16 Enter the information requested about your company pension, if you have one.

17 Click **Next**.

18 Click the arrow up or down ( ) to set the rate of return you expect on your investments while you are still working. The pie chart showing the percentage of your portfolio in different types of asset categories automatically adjusts.

19 Do the same for your post-retirement investments.

20 Click **Next**.

Note: For more information on risk, return, and investment classes, see Chapter 2.

CONTINUED ▶

Of course, these results are not guaranteed. You have made certain assumptions—maybe optimistic ones—about inflation, raises, and returns.

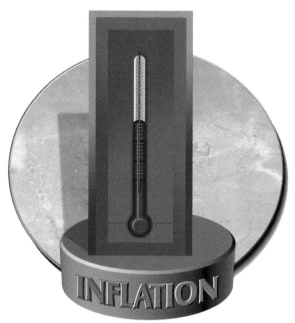

FIND OUT WHAT YOU CAN EXPECT AT RETIREMENT

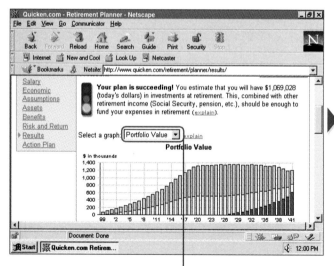

*Note: If the planner gives you the message **Your plan is not succeeding** at this point, skip ahead to the section "Adjust Your Saving and Spending Patterns."*

21 Click the arrow (▼) next to **Portfolio Value** and scroll down to see graphs of your income, savings, and expenses.

22 Click **Next**.

■ This is a summary of the information that was used in calculating your retirement income. You should check all the data to make sure these are the retirement ages, savings rates, and other variables you want.

?

What if a lot of changes take place in my life all at once?

You can redo the calculation as often as you want.

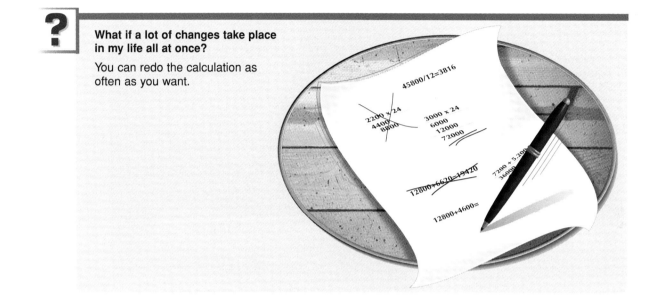

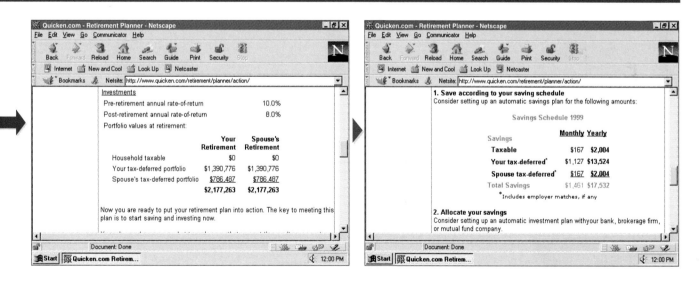

■ A summary of your investments

■ A schedule for saving

ADJUST YOUR SAVING AND SPENDING PATTERNS

If you have followed through the investment plan in the section "Prepare for Retirement by Using a Typical Online Planner," and it looks as if you will not have enough money to retire on, you can try fiddling with some of the assumptions that went into your calculations. Increase your 401(k) contribution, for instance, and your retirement income goes up.

CHANGE YOUR INVESTMENT MIX

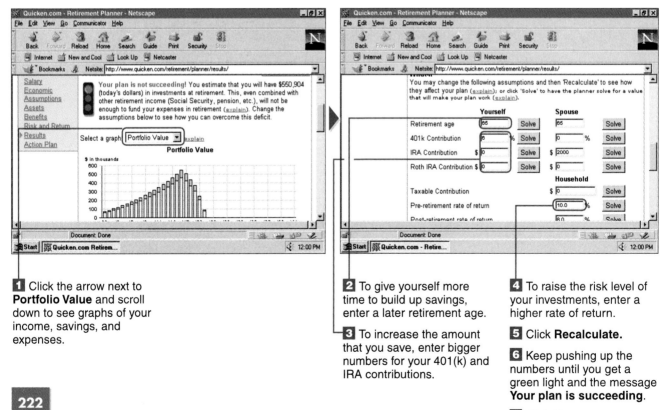

1 Click the arrow next to **Portfolio Value** and scroll down to see graphs of your income, savings, and expenses.

2 To give yourself more time to build up savings, enter a later retirement age.

3 To increase the amount that you save, enter bigger numbers for your 401(k) and IRA contributions.

4 To raise the risk level of your investments, enter a higher rate of return.

5 Click **Recalculate.**

6 Keep pushing up the numbers until you get a green light and the message **Your plan is succeeding**.

7 Click **Next.**

How can I increase the returns from my investments (without looking into a crystal ball)?

Generally, stocks give you higher returns than other standard investments. You can find more advice in Chapter 2.

FIGURE OUT HOW MUCH YOU CAN SAVE IF YOU CURTAIL YOUR SPENDING

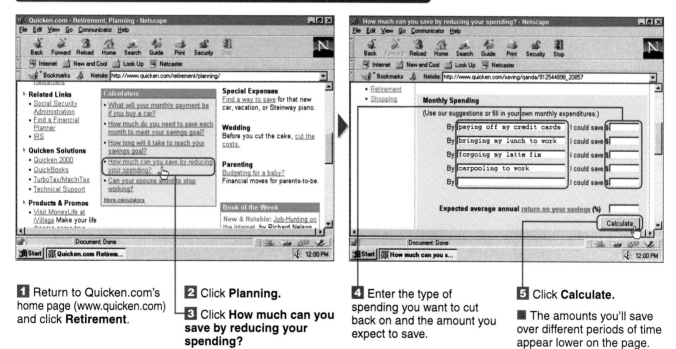

1 Return to Quicken.com's home page (www.quicken.com) and click **Retirement**.

2 Click **Planning.**

3 Click **How much can you save by reducing your spending?**

4 Enter the type of spending you want to cut back on and the amount you expect to save.

5 Click **Calculate.**

■ The amounts you'll save over different periods of time appear lower on the page.

FACTOR UNCERTAINTY INTO YOUR RETIREMENT PLANNING

Many different online programs can help you plan for retirement. One example, **Financial Engines** (www.financialengines.com), **is based on certain classic theories of uncertainty and was developed by Stanford University professor William Sharpe, who won the Nobel Prize in economics in 1990.**

LOG ON TO FINANCIAL ENGINES'S RETIREMENT PLANNER

■ If this is your first time using the site, click **Sign Up** and fill in your personal information on the next few pages.

■ If you have already signed up, enter your user ID and your password. Then click **Login.**

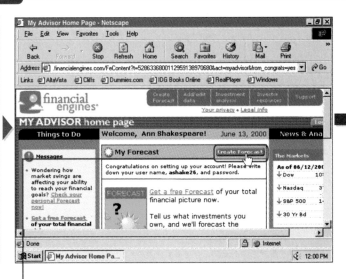

1 Click **Create Forecast** if this is your first time using the site.

If I don't have enough money after I retire, could I go back to work and still collect my pension and Social Security?

You can certainly return to work. Whether you can collect all your retirement benefits, however, depends on your age, whether you're working for the same company or a new one, and whether you completely retired before returning to the work force.

■ If you are a return user and want to add new information, click **Add/Edit Data.**

■ If you are a return user and want to check your forecast, click **Check Your Personal Forecast Now!**

2 Click **Start.**

CONTINUED

FACTOR UNCERTAINTY INTO YOUR RETIREMENT PLANNING (CONTINUED)

You may be surprised at the kind of information that goes into retirement planning.

INPUT BASIC INFORMATION

3 Click **Next.**

4 Enter your birth date by clicking the plus or minus sign (⊞) until you hit the correct month, day, and year.

5 Click **Next.**

Why does my gender matter?

Women tend to outlive men by several years. So they need to build up a bigger retirement nest egg.

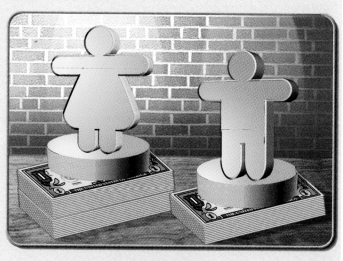

6 Click the circle next to your gender (○ becomes ◉).

7 Click **Next.**

8 Enter your annual income.

9 Click **Next.**

CONTINUED

FACTOR UNCERTAINTY INTO YOUR RETIREMENT PLANNING (CONTINUED)

All retirement planning programs need the same basic data, such as your current income, your age, and the age at which you hope to retire. But they probably focus on different aspects of your current finances and future projections.

INPUT BASIC INFORMATION (CONTINUED)

10 Click the plus or minus sign (⬦) until you reach the state in which you live.

11 Click **Next.**

12 Click the plus or minus sign (⬦) until you reach the desired retirement age.

13 Click **Next.**

How does my marital status affect my retirement plans?

It has two effects: Your spouse may have income and savings to contribute to the mix. And together, you will need enough money for two, not just one.

Financial Engines Investment Advisor ▢▢✕

Enter your marital status

Marital status determines your tax status. If you desire, you may include a spouse or partner in your investment plan. The Advisor considers your total household income when generating your Forecast and giving advice.

Marital status
- ● single
- ○ married
- ○ partner

Get Advice
What's Advice?

Help

Contact Us

Quit

< Back   Next >

Warning: Applet Window
Applet started   🔒 🌐 Internet
🏁 Start | Financial Engines Online I... | Financial Engines Inv...   🔊 12:00 PM

Financial Engines Investment Advisor ▢▢✕

Enter your retirement goal

The amount below is the Advisor's estimate of the annual pre-tax income you will need in retirement to maintain your pre-retirement standard of living. The default has been set to 70% of your projected household income in the year you retire, assuming 1.5% income growth per year above inflation.

Your projected household income at age 65 is $117,037. Your default goal has been set to 70% of that amount, which is $81,000.

Get Advice
What's Advice?

Annual retirement income goal $ ▨81,000 ▴▾

Help

Contact Us

Quit

< Back   Next >

Warning: Applet Window
Applet started   🔒 🌐 Internet
🏁 Start | Financial Engines Online I... | Financial Engines Inv...   🔊 12:00 PM

---

14 Click the circle next to your correct marital status (○ changes to ◉).

15 Click **Next.**

16 If you click **Married** or **Partner**, other screens then ask the same questions about your spouse that were asked about you – birth date, gender, income, planned retirement age, and so on. Fill in the requested information and click **Next** on each screen.

17 Click the plus or minus sign (▴▾) to set your retirement income goal higher or lower. It is preset to 70 percent of your working income – a standard, somewhat conservative assumption.

18 Click **Next.**

19 Click **Next** on the next two screens.

CONTINUED ▶

FACTOR UNCERTAINTY INTO YOUR RETIREMENT PLANNING (CONTINUED)

Financial Engines puts a lot of emphasis on 401(k) plans, because these are becoming the major vehicle through which Americans save for retirement.

INPUT DETAILS ABOUT YOUR 401(K) PLAN

20 Select the type of account to enter, such as **401 (k)** (○ changes to ◉).

21 Click **Next.**

22 Enter the name of your company's 401(k) account.

23 Specify if your job is associated with the account ↳ (○ changes to ◉).

24 Click the circle next to $ or % (○ changes to ◉), and then enter the size of your contribution.

25 Input the after-tax total cost, if you have that information.

26 Click **Next.**

Financial Engines ® and the Financial Engines Investment Advisor [SM] are marks of Financial Engines, Inc. Copyright © 1998–2000. All rights reserved.

230

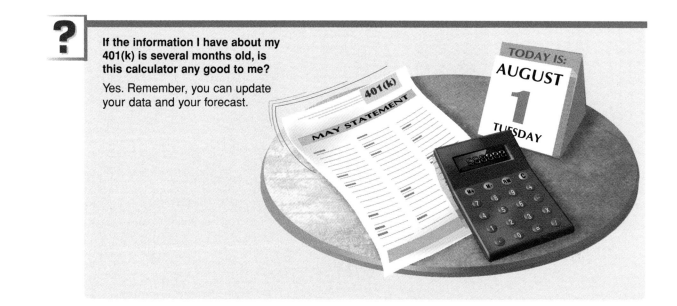

?

If the information I have about my 401(k) is several months old, is this calculator any good to me?

Yes. Remember, you can update your data and your forecast.

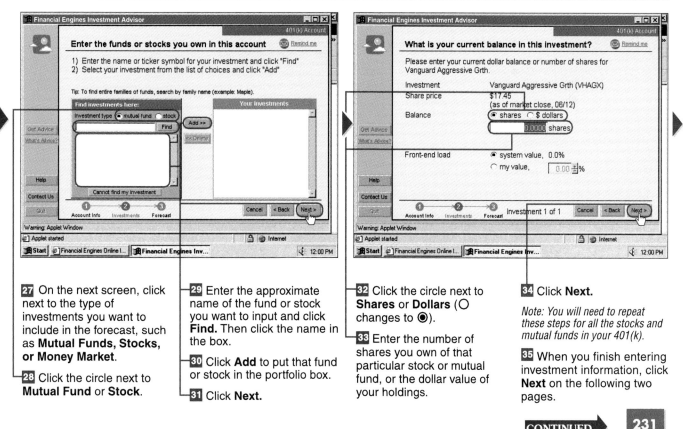

27 On the next screen, click next to the type of investments you want to include in the forecast, such as **Mutual Funds, Stocks, or Money Market**.

28 Click the circle next to **Mutual Fund** or **Stock**.

29 Enter the approximate name of the fund or stock you want to input and click **Find.** Then click the name in the box.

30 Click **Add** to put that fund or stock in the portfolio box.

31 Click **Next.**

32 Click the circle next to **Shares** or **Dollars** (O changes to ◉).

33 Enter the number of shares you own of that particular stock or mutual fund, or the dollar value of your holdings.

34 Click **Next.**

Note: You will need to repeat these steps for all the stocks and mutual funds in your 401(k).

35 When you finish entering investment information, click **Next** on the following two pages.

CONTINUED ▶

FACTOR UNCERTAINTY INTO YOUR RETIREMENT PLANNING (CONTINUED)

Because there is so much uncertainty when you try to project into the future, Financial Engines does not try to tell you precisely how much money you will have when you retire. Rather, it estimates how likely you are to meet your goals.

DETERMINE WHETHER YOU ARE LIKELY TO MEET YOUR RETIREMENT GOALS

36 Click **Finish.**

■ The site will then analyze your information and create your forecast.

37 Check **How much annual income might I expect in retirement?** or **How much might my investments be worth by age 65?** to get those forecasts (○ changes to ◉).

How does this program arrive at its estimations?

The process involves complex mathematical algorithms. But basically, it looks at literally thousands of different possible economic scenarios between now and your planned retirement, including different levels of inflation and interest rates.

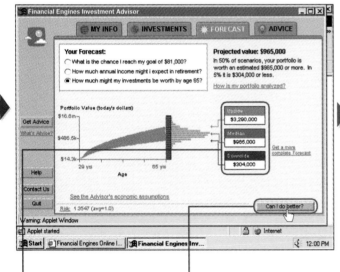

■ When you click the questions about annual income and investments, a box pops up on-screen showing you the high, median, and low amounts you can expect.

38 Click **Can I do better?** to find out how to get specific advice on improving your forecast from Financial Engines.

39 Click **Subscribe** if you would like to receive financial planning recommendations for a fee from Financial Engines.

CHAPTER 11

Watching Out for Danger Spots

What if you press the wrong key? What if a power blackout sends your computer crashing, or a hacker taps into your brokerage account? This chapter gives you some advice on how to keep your sensitive online transactions safe.

AVOID HUMAN ERROR

If trading stocks online with the click of a mouse is easy, then maybe clicking the mouse wrong and messing up a trade is just as easy. But you can protect yourself from your own mistakes.

Here are some common worries:

- When you go online, your transaction is carried out immediately. You can't call back and say to a human being, "Wait, I've changed my mind!"

- Every Web site URL is a unique, complex, and often long chain of numbers and letters in no logical order. You may not even realize that you have typed a URL wrong. But all you need is one digit out of place, and your money could end up in Timbuktu.

- For your protection, most financial sites require you to sign on with a password. What if you forget the password?

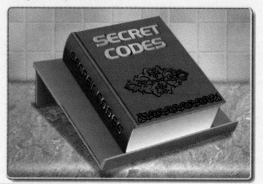

SOLUTION 1: CAREFULLY CHECK WHAT YOU TYPE

A good first step is to go slowly and be extra careful. Before you click Send or press Enter while performing an online transaction, check and recheck to make sure that you have correctly typed the URL, your own online address, and other relevant information. After all, if you were doing the transaction on paper, you would need to proofread your bank account number and the amount of money involved.

Well-designed sites do not process a transaction unless you fill out every required line in the form. However, they have no way of knowing if you fill out the lines correctly.

SOLUTION 2: USE THE BACKUP PASSWORD

The people who create Web sites know that some people inevitably forget their passwords, and they have built in a second line of defense. For example, Yahoo! issues you a new password if you confirm your identity by providing your date of birth. The online auction site eBay (www.ebay.com) sends a new password to you through e-mail. The online retirement planning site Financial Engines Investment Advisor (www.financial engines.com) gives you a choice of topics to use as your backup—your favorite vacation spot, your pet's name, your place of birth, and that perennial favorite, your mother's maiden name.

Okay, now here's the next problem: What if you get a new pet?

You can't really do much damage with just one wrong keystroke or mouse click. It takes a lot more than one stroke, for example, to erase a file or complete a major transaction.

SOLUTION 3: PRACTICE GOING ONLINE

As with most things in life, you will feel more comfortable going online the more you actually try it. Chapter 1 discusses some ways that you can gain Internet experience without any risk.

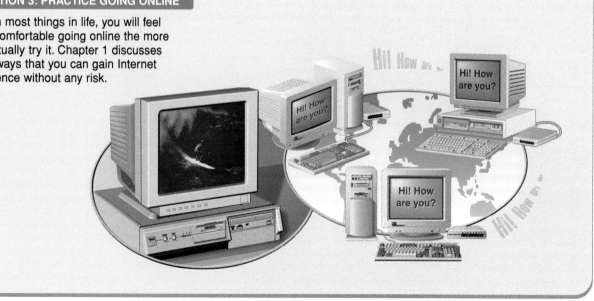

SOLUTION 4: DON'T JUST CLICK YES IN CONFIRMATION DIALOG BOXES

Another way that most sites protect you is with confirmation dialog boxes. Whenever you enter a major transaction—say, to delete a file or to buy a stock—a dialog box pops up on the screen and asks some version of the question: "Are you sure you want to do this?" In fact, you may be asked to confirm your decision more than once. You can see Chapter 9 for some examples of Citibank's (www.citibank.com) confirmation dialog boxes.

In a variation on this idea, many online vendors, such as Amazon.com and the auction site eBay, require you to take two steps to complete a transaction. First, you type the item you want to purchase or the amount you want to bid, and then, separately, you submit the order or bid.

The four tactics discussed in this section all give you a second chance to change your mind or correct or prevent a mistake.

COPE WITH TECHNOLOGICAL BREAKDOWNS

The more complex the technology, the more chances of something malfunctioning. Power blackouts temporarily halted trading at the Pacific Stock Exchange in December 1998 and at the Chicago Board of Trade and the Chicago Board Options Exchange in August 1999. Do you have any defense against technological mayhem?

SOLUTION 1: CONFIRM YOUR TRANSACTION

You can't fix anything until you make sure that a transaction really took place.

E-mail has some protection built in. Your browser usually flashes a message telling you that your e-mail has been sent. That does not mean the message was actually received, but if there was a problem delivering it, the e-mail usually bounces back to your mailbox.

If your bank, broker, or mutual fund does not automatically send you a confirmation that a transaction is complete, you should request one.

SOLUTION 2: MAINTAIN ACCOUNTS WITH MORE THAN ONE BROKER

Chances are, when one broker has problems with its phone lines, Internet access, computers, or some other technical function, other firms do not. So, if you have a second broker, you can quickly shift there to carry out your transaction without delay.

Just in case weather or a local power outage is the problem, you may want to choose brokers in different cities.

You should also trade occasionally through both firms, even if you think one is far and away better at everything. That way you keep up-to-date on changes at each firm.

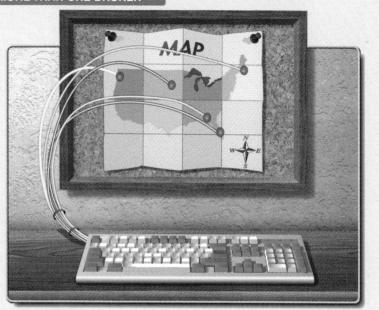

SOLUTION 3: CHOOSE BROKERS WHO ALSO HAVE PHONE AND BRANCH ACCESS

If all the new technology fails, you need to be able to place an order the old-fashioned way—by picking up the telephone or going in person to your broker's office. So select brokers who have that kind of availability.

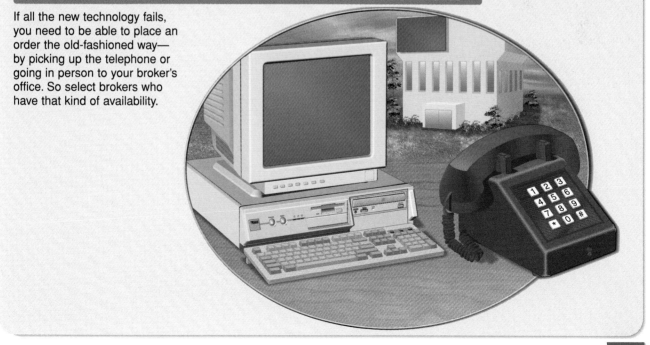

MAKE SURE THAT YOUR TRANSACTIONS ARE SECURE

Chapter 1 explains the public key/private key system that online companies use to encode the financial information you send out via the Net. That is just the first step in protecting your transactions.

Sites that use the double-key coding system display special URL names or icons. This applies to online shopping sites as well as brokerages and banks.

You should see an s after the http in the URL or a little icon of a closed padlock or an old-fashioned key—unbroken— somewhere fairly prominently on the home page. If the site does not have one of those clues, or if the padlock is open or the key is broken, do not use it for any transaction that involves sensitive information.

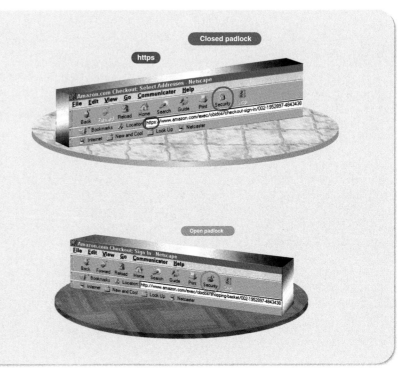

USE FIREWALLS

"In our office," says financial planner Ross Levin of Accredited Investors in Minneapolis, "we've created a separate server (or private network), behind a firewall." A *firewall* is a computer or software that runs security checks on all information passing between a private intranet system and the Internet. Clients of Accredited Investors can connect to the firm's server to do tax calculations, financial planning, and anything else that is handled in-house. No one outside that office can get access to the information. This is similar to the intranet systems many companies have set up for interoffice e-communication.

If a broker, bank, financial planner, or other company you use has such a system, you can perform any transaction it allows in complete confidence without worrying about security breaches of its internal server.

The catch, of course, is that clients on a protected intranet system can only devise investment plans. In order to trade stocks or transfer assets for real, they have to hook up to brokerages and banks on the Internet—at which point the firewall protects them only from incoming information. Their outgoing information must rely on the other security measures discussed in this chapter and in Chapter 1.

GET DISCONNECTED AUTOMATICALLY

Some sites, such as Citibank (www.citibank.com), automatically disconnect you if you do not click the mouse, strike a key on the keyboard, or register any other signs of life on the site for six minutes or so. The reason: What if you had walked away from a computer without logging off? Anyone could come in off the street and, using your login, start taking money out of your bank account or buying and selling stocks in your brokerage account.

Leaving a live online site unprotected is like leaving your wallet on the sidewalk.

MAKE SURE THAT YOUR TRANSACTIONS ARE SECURE (CONTINUED)

Web security may involve good old paper, modern technology, or just a dose of common sense.

CHOOSE A TRULY SECRET PASSWORD

These days, nearly every site asks you to select a secret password or personal identification number (PIN). The best ones are easy for you to remember, but difficult for someone else to guess. For example, you could use the name of your high school boyfriend or girlfriend rather than your spouse's name.

Long passwords with lots of random digits instead of letters are also hard for strangers to guess—but hard for you to remember, too!

Most important: Don't tell anyone your password or PIN, don't store it on your computer, and don't write it down anywhere.

READ STATEMENTS CLOSELY

Keep records of all your transactions. Then, when you get your regular credit card, bank, or brokerage statement, you should look it over with an eagle eye. Is there a charge for a stock trade you never made? Was money electronically withdrawn from your bank account to pay the same bill twice?

RELY ON PAPER AND PHONES

If you are really nervous about security, you can always go the low-tech route. You can ask the Web site that you are dealing with to mail you written confirmation of every transaction. Instead of typing in sensitive data like your Social Security or credit card number, you may be able to submit the information by phone.

Of course, as online experts are quick to point out, communicating by telephone line is actually less secure than going online. After all, phone calls are not normally encrypted in any way.

SECURITY: IS ANY PROTECTION FOOLPROOF?

You've probably heard of *hackers*—computer whizzes who break into Web sites, despite the security measures. How dangerous and prevalent are they? Practically speaking, hacking is still rare.

Web sites that involve financial transactions—such as shopping, banking, and stock trading—have stricter security measures than sites that are just for information, entertainment, or chatting. Chapter 1 explains how Web sites protect the transfer of information with public/private key encryption, and the section "Make Sure That Your Transactions Are Secure" earlier in this chapter mentions some of the signs of security, such as the icon of a closed padlock and https as part of the URL.

CHECKING YOUR BROWSER'S ENCRYPTION LEVEL

Netscape Communicator 4.72 and
Internet Explorer 5 have 128-bit
encryption available, which is a very high
level of coding that can keep your
sensitive online transactions secure. To
check whether your browser has this level
of protection, go to the About option
under the Help menu.

If your browser doesn't have 128-bit
encryption, the About or Security option
probably has information on how to
download a program that will upgrade
your browser to this level of protection.
(You can also find information about
downloading encryption-level upgrades
from the Web site for your browser—such
as www.microsoft.com or
www.netscape.com.)

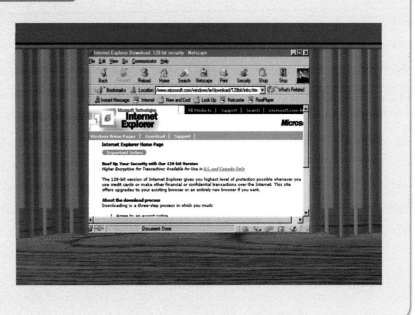

HOW HACKERS HELP

Believe it or not, hackers can sometimes
be a business's best friend! They show
the Web site's security team the
weaknesses in the site's security system,
letting the developers know exactly what
to fix. In fact, some companies have
actually hired hackers specifically to test
their security measures by trying to
break in.

PROTECT YOUR PRIVACY

You may not realize how much personal information you give away—or what is done with it—every time you sign up for a new Web site, trade a stock online, or order a purchase electronically.

WHAT SECRETS ARE YOU REVEALING?

In order to register with Yahoo! for e-mail, chat rooms, and message boards, for example, you must provide your birth date, gender, zip code, occupation, and hobbies. If you shop online, you are telling the site your credit card number, e-mail address, home address, and a bit about your tastes or interests. If you are doing financial planning, you are revealing much more—including your age, your salary, and the amount of money in your retirement accounts and how it is invested.

WHAT CAN A SITE DO WITH YOUR INFORMATION?

Most often, sites use the information they collect to target ads, promotions, or personalized services, such as weather reports, to you. They may also share the information with telemarketers and other third parties.

For now, very few U.S. laws protect the integrity of online information. The Children's Online Privacy Protection Act of 1998, which forbids Web sites from collecting data about children under 13 without parents' permission, is probably the only one of significance. But the industry has mostly been allowed to regulate itself. European laws, meanwhile, tend to be stricter.

HOW IS A WEB SITE SELLING YOUR INFORMATION DIFFERENT FROM WHAT TELEMARKETERS DO?

Merchants have been selling their customer lists to direct marketers for years, of course, even before there was an Internet. What makes online data collection more worrisome is that it involves so much more information and such personal information.

DO ONLINE SITES TELL YOU WHEN THEY COLLECT INFORMATION?

When the Federal Trade Commission surveyed 1,400 commercial sites in 1998, it found that only 14 percent let users know what they did with the personal information they amassed. By all accounts, that percentage has risen since. The most thorough sites tell users what kind of personal and identifiable information they collect, how it is used, with whom they share it, how they keep it secure, and what choice—if any—users have in any of this.

That still means that many sites keep their customers in the dark, however. And some consumer advocates say that merely telling users that information is being collected is not enough. These advocates say that consumers should have the same rights they've fought to gain regarding their credit records: They should be able to see the actual information that's collected and given out—their occupation, hobbies, zip code, and whatever else—so that they can correct any mistakes.

Internet privacy has become a major issue in American politics and in international trade. For example, it is still a subject of debate which country's privacy laws apply when an online business in the United States sells goods to someone in Europe.

Large technology companies have formed at least two lobbying groups in the United States to try to weaken any potential privacy regulations or legislation.

HOW CAN YOU FIND OUT WHAT A SITE DOES WITH YOUR PERSONAL INFORMATION?

Some Web sites have a link to their privacy policy somewhere on their home page. One example is on Quicken's site (www.quicken.com); the link **Your Privacy Rights** is toward the bottom of the page.

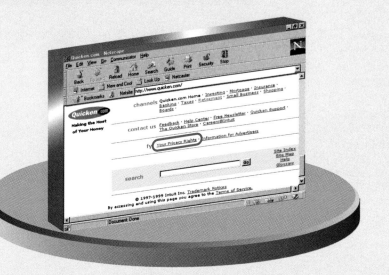

Click **Your Privacy Rights**

DOESN'T ENCRYPTION PROTECT YOU?

True, the information you send out when you trade a stock or pay your bills is probably protected by the public key/private key encryption method discussed in Chapter 1. But that only protects you against break-ins. It does not stop the Web site from collecting the less-sensitive information that you've inputted, such as your zip code, birth date, gender, and e-mail address, and using it for other purposes—even without your explicit authorization.

WHAT CAN YOU DO TO PROTECT YOURSELF?

You can often "opt out" of certain information-sharing. However, that may mean also losing out—for example, on promotions and access to e-mail and chat rooms.

You can also safeguard yourself by following the recommendations in this chapter.

WHAT ARE COOKIES?

Essentially, *cookies* are used to create an electronic tracking system. Each cookie is a small bit of text—invisible to you—that certain Web sites store on your computer when you visit them. The sites can then note each time you log on and what you did.

The use of cookies may make you think that Big Brother is watching you, but Web site administrators maintain that their purpose is purely commercial. For example, say that you shop at an online bookstore with a cookie: The next time you visit that site, the site may remember the books you browsed and greet with you some similar titles you may like, if its cookie is set up to track this type of information. The cookie can also help merchants target their marketing.

If you're concerned about cookies, you can set your browser to refuse them, but that may make it difficult to continue some transactions. Anyway, you have some protection, because only the site that creates a cookie can access it.

KEEP YOUR BROKER HONEST

The U.S. Securities and Exchange Commission (SEC), along with several other government agencies, regulates brokers and the securities markets under laws first written in the Depression. Now, many officials say that updated rules are needed to cover online trading.

Because the laws are still in flux, you need to take some extra steps to protect yourself from disreputable brokers. Ask your broker the questions in this section.

IS YOUR BROKER UNDER INVESTIGATION?

Late in 1999, the SEC and New York State Attorney General Eliot Spitzer issued reports pointing out a number of problems with online brokerages. Among other criticisms, the reports said that some brokerages

- Don't fully inform investors of the risks of computer system breakdowns.

- Give investors the false impression that all trades are executed faster than they really are.

- Fail to enforce requirements that limit the amount investors are allowed to trade, based on what kinds of accounts they have and how much credit they have.

You can find out whether the SEC has taken enforcement actions against your broker and what the actions are by going to the SEC's Web site (www.sec.gov) and clicking on **Enforcement Division** and then **Search SEC Information**.

U.S. SECURITIES AND EXCHANGE COMMISSION

"We are the investor's advocate."
William O. Douglas
SEC Chairman, 1937-1939

DOES YOUR BROKER ACCURATELY KEEP TRACK OF YOUR AVAILABLE FUNDS?

Because online investors tend to trade more frequently than others, brokers need to keep a close watch on how much money their customers have available. If they do not, investors can end up buying more on margin than they are supposed to—essentially, going over their credit limit. Yet the SEC's and New York Attorney General's reports found that firms do not always update their accounts frequently enough.

DOES YOUR BROKER PROVIDE THE BEST EXECUTION?

The price of a trade involves more than just matching the bid and offer prices of buyer and seller. The trade also has to be executed promptly, while the price is still available. This is particularly important in online trading, because speed is one of the reasons investors turn to the Internet.

Thus, a brokerage can badly hurt its customers if it uses an incompetent firm to execute trades.

Another practice of unscrupulous brokers is *front-running,* which is when a firm hears about a good price on a stock and makes a trade for its own account instead of performing its customers' trades first. By the time the firm gets around to taking care of its customers' trades, the bargain price may be gone.

DOES YOUR BROKER CHECK THAT YOUR INVESTMENTS ARE SUITABLE?

One of the key federal securities laws requires brokers to make sure that the investments their customers choose are suitable for their financial circumstances.

Online firms often argue that this law does not apply to them because they don't get involved in selecting investments. These firms say that their investors make their own decisions, using the brokerage sites only to carry out the trade.

But the SEC points out that online brokerages do more than merely follow orders. Many offer original research or send targeted e-mails alerting customers to news about investments they may be interested in. And some, such as Merrill Lynch and Morgan Stanley Dean Witter, provide advice to certain online investors, as discussed in Chapter 3.

Eventually, the issue will probably be resolved by an SEC or court ruling.

BE CAREFUL WITH TIPS FROM MESSAGE BOARDS AND CHAT ROOMS

Message boards and chat rooms are forums in which Web surfers casually exchange ideas, complaints, advice, tips, and gossip—about anything: a particular stock, an investing strategy, some recent news headline, or, of course, nothing to do with finance at all. You can usually find message boards and chat rooms on America Online, on portals like Yahoo!, and for financial topics, on sites that offer financial news and advice, such as **TheStreet.com** (www.thestreet.com) and **Motley Fool** (www.fool.com).

These sites can be fun, like chatting with your friends. But they are no substitute for research.

READ AND POST MESSAGES ON THE MOTLEY FOOL MESSAGE BOARD

1 At Motley Fool (www.fool.com), click **Discussion Boards**.

2 Click **Best Of**.

Should I act on tips I get from a message board or chat room?

Only if you have other reasons for doing so. After all, most of the people on these sites are ordinary investors just like you. They have no special knowledge about the stocks they discuss.

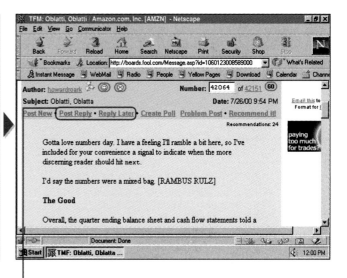

3 Click on a topic.

4 If you want to reply, click **Post Reply** or **Reply Later**.

CONTINUED

BE CAREFUL WITH TIPS FROM MESSAGE BOARDS AND CHAT ROOMS (CONTINUED)

Message boards and chat rooms can be useful for collecting anecdotal evidence. If you have suspicions about a particular investment, ask if anyone else in the chat room has had a problem with the company—and see what kind of reactions you get!

CHAT IN AN AOL CHAT ROOM

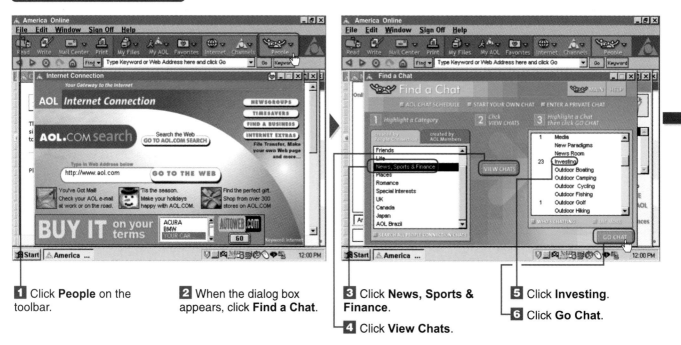

1 Click **People** on the toolbar.

2 When the dialog box appears, click **Find a Chat**.

3 Click **News, Sports & Finance**.

4 Click **View Chats**.

5 Click **Investing**.

6 Click **Go Chat**.

?

How do people misuse chat rooms and message boards?

Here is a typical example: In December 1999, two men were arrested in California for allegedly posting hundreds of fake messages on several message boards, claiming that an obscure, bankrupt company whose stock they owned was about to be acquired. Other online users, thinking the messages came from a lot of interested investors, hurried to buy the worthless stock.

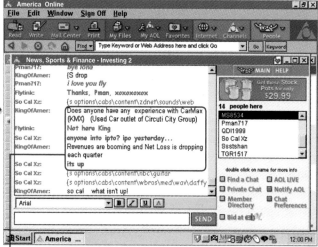

■ Some chat about stocks, including MU (Micron Technology, a computer and integrated circuit manufacturer), RHAT (Red Hat, distributor of the popular Red Hat Linux operating system), BeOS (BE Inc., a developer of operating systems), and WHIT (Whittman-Hart, a high-tech consultant)

■ More chatting about stocks

AVOID ONLINE SCAMS

Sometimes, it seems as if online investing attracts more crooks and con artists than any other line of business. Government regulators say that this is mainly because it is so easy to hide your identity while manipulating a stock price. This means that when you invest online, you need to take extra precautions to make sure a proposed investment is legitimate.

STEERING CLEAR OF CLASSIC FRAUDS

Of course, you can find the standard scams on the Internet as well as in a broker's office. These include *pyramid schemes*, in which each new investor's money goes only to pay the earlier investors, not to actually invest in anything. Another classic tactic is to rake in assets for a nonexistent entity. For example, the SEC in early 1999 shut down a site that was selling unregistered bonds for "New Utopia," a tax haven that was supposedly going to be built in the middle of the Caribbean Sea on a giant concrete platform.

To avoid classic frauds, first, do basic research about any investment you're considering. In Chapter 4, you can get some advice about the type of information to look for and where to find it. In the example of the New Utopia bonds, if you did some simple research, you would quickly discover that there is no such country.

Second, you should be especially wary of dealing with any entity you've never heard of. That applies to the brokers you invest with as well as the companies or governments you invest in. After all, when you invest online, you can't just drop in on the home office.

RECOGNIZING PHONY WEB POSTINGS

In April 1999, many investors clicked on to what they thought was a news story about a stock called *PairGain Technologies* from the Web site of the Bloomberg news service. Unfortunately, the article turned out to be only a very good imitation of a Bloomberg story. But those who rushed to buy the stock based on the story were taken on a ride up to $11.25 per share and then down to $9.38 when the hoax was discovered.

Because it's relatively easy to create a Web site (it's certainly easier than printing an entire newspaper!), it is also easy for crooks to create misleading Web sites.

A phony site, if done well, can be hard to catch. You may be able to test a site's validity by trying its links. If the site has a story pretending to be from another site, as in the Bloomberg case, you can call the public relations department of the company that the story is about or contact the site it purportedly comes from. Some experts suggest that sham sites are often shabbier than real ones, but the SEC also points out that often just the opposite is true.

Legitimate   Scam

IGNORING DOT-COM HYPE

Investors cannot seem to get enough of companies that claim to be connected to the Internet—companies whose names often end with "dot-com." But having a business that involves the Internet is no guarantee of a glorious future. Take one example from the files of FinancialWeb's Stock Detective (www.stockdetective.com): Digitcom Corp., which claimed to have a deal to provide Internet-based telephone service to part of the former Soviet Union. The deal may have sounded promising, but the company's financial condition apparently wasn't. The Securities and Exchange Commission temporarily halted trading in the stock in July 1999 because, as the SEC put it, "questions have been raised about the adequacy and accuracy of publicly disseminated information . . . related to the company's financial condition."

This case of Digitcom is a good example of why you should always check the SEC's postings of companies under investigation at its Web site www.sec.gov. But to catch the suspicious companies before they get as far as an SEC investigation, you need to do the kind of basic research discussed in Chapter 4.

And of course, don't be fooled by the aura of the Net. Some Internet-related stocks actually have crashed. Even many of the most successful Internet companies have yet to make their first dime of profit.

REPORT AND TRACK ONLINE SCAMS

Luckily, if the Web has brought us new scams, it has also brought new sites that track online fraud. One of them is the National Fraud Information Center (NFIC) at www.fraud.org.

REPORT AND GET INFORMATION ABOUT FRAUD AT THE NFIC

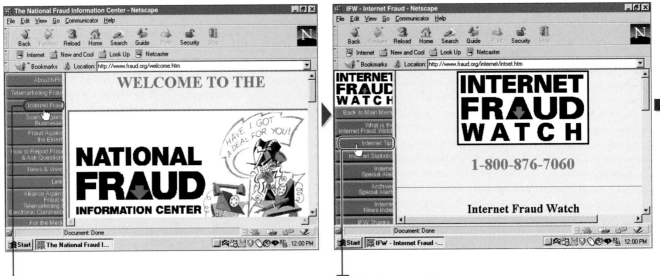

1 At the National Fraud Information Center (www.fraud.org), click **Internet Fraud**.

2 Click **Internet Tips**.

?

Is there a central listing of all known online scams?

The National Fraud Information Center posts all the reports it collects on a national fraud database. Because that database is open only to law enforcement personnel, you can't use it to check out suspicious offers yourself. But at least you can report your own experiences, for government officials to investigate.

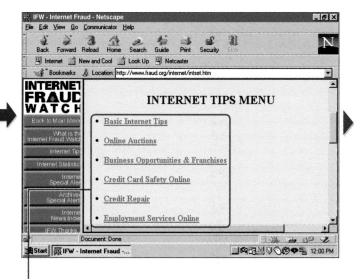

3 Click any type of fraud you want to learn about or scroll down to report a fraud.

■ Among the site's tips: Find out where your cyberspace company is really located; be wary of "hot" tips from a chat room or message board; and

don't give out sensitive information, such as your bank account number, unless you're sure the company is legitimate.

4 If on the Internet Tips page you chose to scroll down to report a fraud, click **How to Report Fraud & Ask Questions**.

CONTINUED

REPORT AND TRACK ONLINE SCAMS (CONTINUED)

In 1998 the Securities and Exchange Commission created a special Office of Internet Enforcement. The agency files more than 30 cases of online fraud per year, on average.

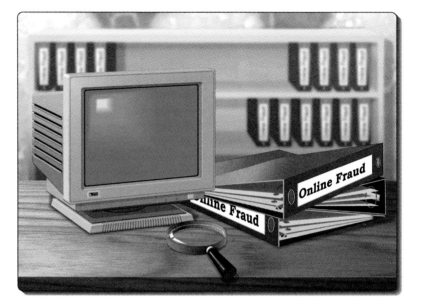

GET ADVICE FROM THE SEC

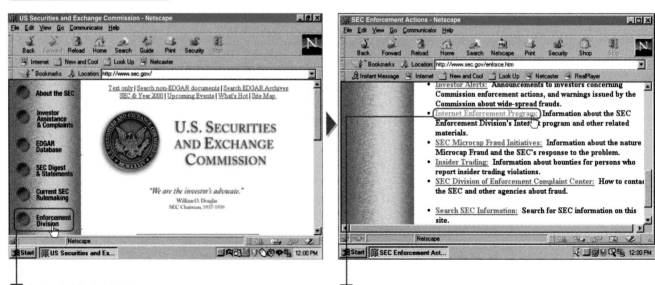

1 At the SEC's Web site (www.sec.gov), click **Enforcement Division**.

2 Scroll down and click **Internet Enforcement Program** for a list of recent investigations.

How can I tell if an online investment is a scam?

Here's the best advice, in a nutshell: If an investment sounds too good to be true, it probably is. Avoid it.

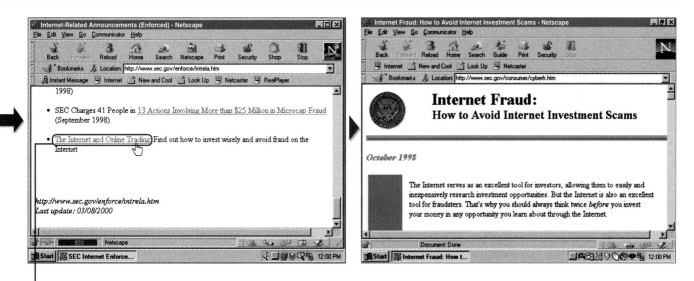

3 Scroll down to and click **The Internet and Online Trading**.

4 On the next page, click **Internet Fraud: How to Avoid Internet Investment Scams**.

■ The SEC's advice for Internet investors is pretty much the same as for all investors: Do your homework; don't let yourself get pressured; and be wary of words like *guarantee, high return,* and *limited offer.*

CHAPTER 12

Now a Word about Day Trading

How is day trading different from other trading? Why is it considered risky? This chapter shows you how day trading works and some ways to minimize the risk.

WHAT IS DAY TRADING?

Essentially, *day trading* means jumping in and out of stocks nonstop all day long—and then selling out completely by the time the markets close.

Most day trading is done online—but *not all online trading is day trading!*

ONE-MINUTE OWNERSHIP

Day traders are constantly buying and selling stocks because they hope to move just before the prices are about to rise or fall. They may own their shares for no more than a few minutes or even seconds.

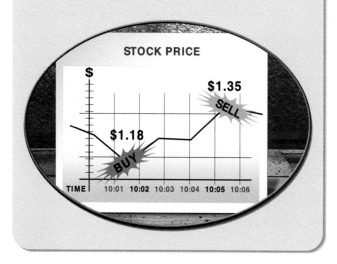

THE IMPORTANCE OF TECHNOLOGY

It's hard to imagine day trading without the Internet. Day traders spend their time surfing the Net, trying to grab the newest tips from online headlines or chat rooms. They also do their trades online—often from their homes, but sometimes secretly at work.

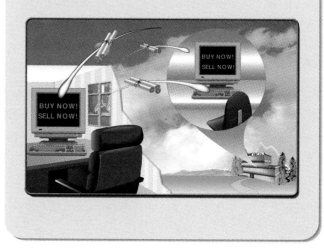

DAY TRADING VERSUS INVESTING

All investors buy and sell, hoping to buy at the lowest price and sell at the highest. What is so different about day traders?

HOW LONG THE INVESTORS STICK AROUND

Unlike day traders, traditional investors have patience. They know that stocks go up and down, and they are willing to wait out a bad stretch. They could hold a stock for decades. Traditional investors certainly keep their shares overnight.

Day traders almost always sell their stock the same day—or even the same hour—that they buy it.

HOW THE INVESTORS MAKE THEIR DECISIONS

Traditional investors do a lot of research before deciding to buy or sell an investment. They look at the company's products, history, balance sheet, and competitive situation within its industry—the kind of information described in Chapter 4.

Day traders do not have time for that. Although they may try to keep up with some financial journals and news shows, they're moving too fast to catch much more than a headline. Their main research tool is the stock chart.

UNDERSTAND THE DANGERS OF DAY TRADING

Day trading is very, very risky. Most experts say that 90 percent of day traders lose money.

WARNING: Because day trading is so risky, it is definitely not for beginning or conservative investors. Remember that with day trading you have a very high likelihood of losing your money.

IS DAY TRADING AN ADDICTION?

Certainly, day trading resembles gambling or drug abuse in many ways. Like addicts, traders often tell themselves: "Just one more try. This next stock will be my lucky break." The more they lose, the more determined they become to try again in order to make up the loss.

The excitement and speed of day trading can also be a lot like the high that people get from drugs.

YOU'RE FLYING BLIND

You could think of a day trader as a pilot flying an airplane blindfolded. Day traders do not research the routes they take. They count on a combination of luck and split-second timing to avoid crashing.

YOU PAY FOR EVERY TRADE

Every time you buy or sell a security, you pay a transaction fee. So the more often you buy and sell, the more you pay in fees. With day traders making perhaps hundreds of trades each day, those fees can add up quickly.

THE PRICE MOVES FASTER THAN YOU CAN

Day trading is based on speed. The basic strategy is to get into a stock just before it goes up and get out just before it drops. As soon as traders sniff what they think is a hint that something is about to happen, they punch in their trade.

The problem is, no matter how fast day traders punch their keyboards and no matter how many trades they make per hour, they still have to wait for their trade to be executed. In that time delay, the price is likely to move without them.

IS DAY TRADING RIGHT FOR YOU?

Despite the terrible odds, a few people do manage to make some money—or at least, tread water—by day trading. Take this quiz to see if you could be one of them.

HOW TO READ THE QUIZ RESULTS

If you answer yes to three or fewer questions, you are the wrong type of person to day trade. You would be better off doing some research and buying stocks the traditional way.

If you answer yes to four or five questions, you have some of the qualities needed for day trading, but you are still hesitant. You might try it just for a day or two.

If you answer yes to six or more questions, you are probably itching to do it. Go ahead. But you will undoubtedly still lose money.

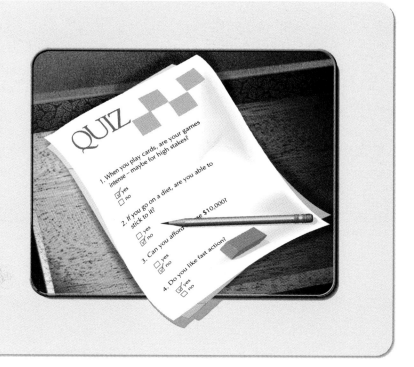

A DAY TRADING QUIZ

1. When you play cards, are your games intense—maybe for high stakes?

2. If you go on a diet, are you able to stick to it?

3. Can you afford to lose $10,000?

4. Do you like fast action?

5. Are you under age 30?

6. Do you have time during the day to watch the markets?

7. Do you like to make decisions promptly, without mulling them over and over?

8. Are you in good health (especially in terms of any heart conditions)?

TIP 1: SET SOME RULES FOR YOURSELF

The best investors always have a strategy. They set rules for themselves and make sure that they follow them.

If you are determined to try day trading, here are a few rules that may save you some grief and money. For that matter, even ordinary investors may find a lot of this advice useful.

ESTABLISH A LIMIT—AND STICK TO IT

Day traders don't use traditional strategies, such as buying only stocks with a certain ratio of price to earnings, because that takes time and research. Instead, day trading strategy involves automatic *limits* and *triggers*. For example, you could promise yourself that you won't buy a particular stock if it goes over a certain price. If your promise is to get out when the stock hits 60, then get out! Be disciplined!

Another strategy: Determine how much you are willing to lose per day and stop trading if you reach that limit.

Because day trading is so much like gambling, you can also try a tactic that some gamblers use to control their losses. Set aside just a small portion of your total investments for day trading—and do all your day trading through a separate broker. That way, even if you lose your entire day trading kitty, the rest of your investments will be safely walled off.

You think you have just heard about a terrific stock. Your brother-in-law has a friend whose barber told him about a customer who works for a company with this great new product. . . .

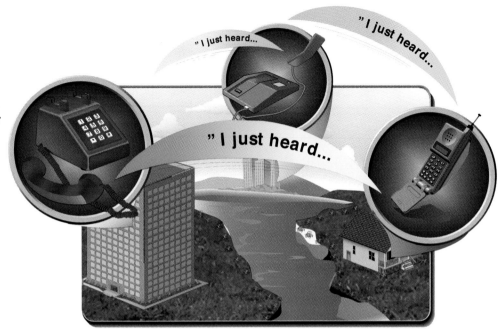

"I just heard...

"I just heard...

"I just heard...

GOSSIP IS NOT A TRADING STRATEGY

Unfortunately, most "tips" like the one your brother-in-law heard turn out to be useless. First of all, too many things can go wrong when you rely on gossip. Perhaps the customer does not really work for the company in question, or the barber heard him incorrectly. Your brother-in-law may have exaggerated.

Besides, if a stock is that great, other investors have probably heard about it, too. This is especially true if your tip came from a public forum like a chat room. Professionals who spend their careers visiting factories, talking to managers, and poring over data may indeed uncover undiscovered gems. But it is very hard for an ordinary investor to do so—especially a day trader who does no research.

HOT TIP

Great new company is selling 30% of their stock. Double your money in 2 days! CALL!!!

555-4137

LOST CAT

Please call:

BEST BUY!
Brand new fridge!
Call for more info!

555-2127

BABYSITTER WA

Two days a
from 8:
to 5:

TIP 3: TAKE YOUR TIME

The last thing a day trader wants to do is slow down for anything. That includes reading the screen or looking at the keyboard. However, if he doesn't slow down and check what he's doing, he could make some costly mistakes.

PICKING THE WRONG NAME

Obviously, you should make sure the stock you are buying is actually the one you want to buy. Because stocks use abbreviation known as *ticker symbols*, too many stock names can look similar if you do not look closely.

If you plan to buy 100 shares of FMC (the giant Chicago-based chemical and machinery conglomerate), you would probably be a little surprised if instead you ended up holding 100 shares of FCM (Franklin Telecommunications, a small communications-equipment maker based in California).

PRESSING THE WRONG KEY

When your fingers are flying over the keyboard, you can too easily hit the wrong letter. That's a particularly serious problem for day traders, who type faster than most people probably talk! If day traders hit the wrong letter or number, they may buy the wrong stock or too much of the right stock.

TIP 4: DON'T JUMP ON A SHOOTING STOCK

When "everyone else" is buying the newest hot stock and its price seems to double by the day, it is hard not to join the mad stampede. What if you stayed away, and it turned out to be the next Microsoft?

However, there are some important reasons to be wary of hotshot stocks that are shooting up unbelievably fast.

TOO LATE

If a stock has been zooming rapidly, you know that you have already missed out on significant gains. By buying now, you're paying a premium price for past history. True, the stock may have some more growth left in it yet, but the chances are not good.

After all, bull markets—that is, strong markets with rising prices—do not last forever. And rare is the company that doesn't hit a plateau in terms of market share, product development, or earnings growth sooner or later.

TOO MUCH HYPE

A burst of publicity may temporarily send a stock price up. But too often, the publicity is based more on wishful thinking than solid facts. When the wishes fail to come true and investors focus on the facts, the stock is likely to sink.

TIP 5: USE LIMIT ORDERS, NOT MARKET ORDERS

Would you go to an auction and say to the auctioneer, "I will top the highest price you are offered for this painting—no matter how high"? Well, that is essentially what you are doing when you place your stock bid with a market order.

SETTING A CEILING

A *market order* is like a blank check. It says that you will pay any amount for the stock, no matter how high its price is.

By contrast, with a *limit order,* you are telling your broker the maximum price you will pay for a stock. That at least gives you some control over how much you will be risking.

DECIDING HOW MUCH YOU WANT THE STOCK

Ultimately, you have to decide if the stock you want is so wonderful that it is worth buying at any price. If the answer is no—and most often, it will be—don't use a market order.

TIP 6: HAVE A BACKUP BROKER

A broker is a day trader's primary tool. If a chef has more than one pot and an architect has more than one pencil, then a day trader can have more than one broker.

IN CASE OF BREAKDOWN

The main advantage of hiring multiple brokers is to have a second shot at trading if your primary broker has technical difficulties. Because day trading depends on technology and speed, it can be a catastrophe if your broker's computer crashes.

For extra protection, make sure that one of your brokers can be reached without using the Internet, such as by phone.

FOR MORE OPTIONS

You may want to choose two brokers with different specialties—a discount broker to save you money on trades you feel sure of and a full-service broker for the times you want advice.

TIP 7: KEEP TRACK OF YOUR PERFORMANCE

Day traders are so busy buying and selling that they do not have time to figure out how they are really doing. But they need to track their performance to find out just how much their habit is costing them.

COMPARING YOURSELF TO OTHERS

If the rest of the stock market has barely registered any gains, and you have made $500 on $5000 worth of trades, then your performance is pretty good. But if the broad markets are up 24 percent, you have actually lost money. You would have done better putting your cash in an index fund or any number of other investments.

So you need to make a chart of every stock and bond you have traded online, showing its price movement, how much you paid for it, and how much you sold it for. Then chart your stocks' ups and downs against the Standard & Poor's 500 stock index (the most commonly followed gauge of the broad stock market) or some other appropriate benchmark.

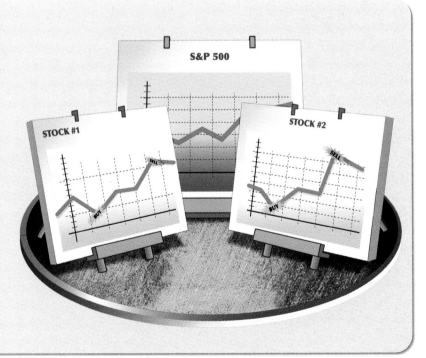

CHECKING THE ONES THAT GOT AWAY

You should also try to find out what happened to some of your stocks after you sold them. If their price dropped, you can pat yourself on the back. But if more of them went up than down, you have to start wondering if you have been too impatient, too quick to sell. The day traders' credo about selling out before the close of day could have hurt you, too.

PAYING THE PRICE

When tracing gains and losses, do not forget what you had to pay in order to trade the stock. At $10 to $15 per trade or even more—the typical price range—these costs can take a big bite out of what you thought were your profits.

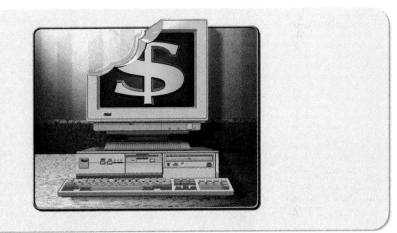

SPENDING HOURS WORKING

And here is one last reason to maintain all these records and charts: Considering that you may have thousands of trades to keep track of for each week, the record-keeping will be enormous.

Does that sound more like a reason why you *wouldn't* want to keep records? That's precisely the point. Instead, it's a reason not to day trade in the first place. (Keeping all these records may be so taxing that you'd decide the work is not worth the time and you'd quit day trading.)

INDEX

INDEX

INDEX